To Angie with love,

DwS

9/0u

Is There a
GOD
For Each of Us?

Dick Levin

Contributing Editor: Ron Levin

ISBN Number: 1-57087-652-5

Library of Congress Control Number: 2004104049

Professional Press
Chapel Hill, NC 27515-4371

Manufactured in the United States of America
04   05   06   07   08   10   9   8   7   6   5   4   3   2   1

Dedicated to my brother, Ron,
whose intellect, faith, drive and imagination
have positively affected the lives of so many people.

CONTENTS

CHAPTER 1

WHY WRITE A BOOK LIKE THIS?

"It'll never get off the ground."

Despite having heard this more times than they wanted to, in 1903, Wilbur and Orville chose the 17th of December and the sand dunes of North Carolina's Outer Banks as the right time and place to take to the air, their first powered flight lasting just 12 seconds. They handily eclipsed my record of just under one second, set 30 years later, when I jumped out of a willow tree in a New Jersey back yard and almost killed myself trying to fly.

No matter—the bug had bitten. I started building model airplanes from the time I could read the plans. I can still smell the dope (the stuff in the little bottle) and the banana oil. When I turned eight, my father took me to the Camden airport for a ride in a Stinson Reliant. The prop spun, the single engine belched huge clouds of blue smoke, and my heart quickened. It was what psychologists like to call a defining moment; and from that day on, though I played with bicycles, roller skates, scooters and toy trains, my heart and soul belonged to flying.

Years later, I fulfilled my dream of majoring in aeronautical engineering in college. Good grades were no problem, but keeping up my enthusiasm was; accordingly, I shifted into another engineering field. Then came an M.S. degree in engineering, a brief professional career, a mandatory stint in the military, all this followed by a Ph.D. in economics and business administration. Bottom line: your author spent the next 30 years teaching MBA's how to run companies and serving as the honcho of UNC's executive education programs. A good, solid, satisfying gig.

Did I mention writing? At first, it was academic—a dozen or so texts on subjects which you probably don't want to know about. Deterministic processes, queuing theory, linear programming...you can't say I didn't warn you. Other titles followed, written about the "real world," one of which got me on the TV talk show circuit, much to my publisher's delight. I recall one of these in particular, on a morning in Dallas. I came on and did seven minutes right after another Orville, this one named Redenbacher, the popcorn king with the polka-dot bow tie. Other books followed, my last one covering my flying a small airplane around the world. Maybe Wilbur and the other Orville were out there—or up there—watching.

At the conclusion of all these years of living, family rearing, flying, reading, writing, teaching and the like, if you took my knowledge of God and religion and put it into a thimble, you'd have room left over for an avocado and a press agent's heart. And there you have it—my first confession!

So why a book about God?

If you're not saying it, you're probably thinking it.

My credentials, you've already heard about, and they hardly qualify me for this subject matter. Then, whence cometh the *chutzpah* needed to attempt this daredevil feat? In a way, it's like jumping out of that tree all over again. Enough of that—let's try picking up the story line in a small town in eastern North

Carolina—the summer of '40. We arrived on the scene with a name no one could pronounce, a religion nobody understood and an accent that generated squints and chuckles. There were four Jewish families, and lest I forget, a small contingent of Ku Kluxers whose fondness for sheets with holes in them is legendary.

Twice a year, the Levins schlepped (a good Yiddish word) 50 miles to the town of Rocky Mount to honor Rosh Hashanah and Yom Kippur—the Jewish New Year and Day of Atonement. A group of men dressed in black conducted the worship services with chants, droning voices and long faces, and the religious ritual that unfolded was mystifying and seemingly interminable. Somehow, though, I sensed this was "important stuff," thus, my younger brother and I tried not to squirm on those hard seats, knowing that if we did, it would merit a painful pinch from our watchful mother. Time passed with college coming not a yawn too soon. Now I could forget all about religion and concentrate on what really mattered, my first true love. Engineering!

Marriage came, and as you might expect, was followed by kids. From age 30 to 50, I was a leader in our Chapel Hill-Durham Reform Jewish temple, heavy on administrative, with an occasional chug-a-lug of new "God lite." My wife, Charlotte, and I went to services fairly regularly, along with our children. I was asked to serve as the president, helped build the first sanctuary and knew enough Hebrew to be a literate participant. But all the while I never questioned what I was doing. Sure, I read the prayers but steered clear of discussion groups. I guess you'd have to say I took God for granted. I almost said "I took God on faith," but we're not ready for that word. Yet.

Early 90's brought retirement. My brain needed stoking, and I consulted for several interesting companies, read lots of books (most of them non-business) and spent more time with friends and family. Gradually, I found myself confronting some of life's core issues: namely, who I was and who was God. (Gulp!) In fairness, up until then my life had been so filled with my vocation, parental assignments and other pursuits, that God had simply not entered into the equation. In sum, it was easier for me to ponder something like say, the financial capitalization of companies than to wrestle with the subject of God. That's not a cop out—it's just the way I was wired. I was a certifiable, card-carrying left brainer. Engineers prefer the predictable, the known, the easily identifiable—something you can pin down in an equation, and I wasn't any different. I wouldn't exactly call it being stupid—just very, very focused. And zooming in on God was way down on my list of priorities. So now you're starting to get some idea of how your author's mind works, which is essential if we're going to have what amounts to a very lengthy and in-depth conversation. Just the two of us—well, actually, the three of us…you, me and God.

By the way, before we go any further, please know this book is written for readers of all ages, faiths, denominations, religious persuasions, belief systems and cultural backgrounds. The only limiting qualifiers are that you enjoy both learning and reading.

A friend opens a door.

Or maybe it was a window.

Probably the latter because it let in some light. He suggested I read a book on early biblical history. I hid a smirk and stifled a yawn, then out of what must have been pure perversity—is there such a thing?—turned to page one. To my surprise, I found it…well, interesting. Actually, more than interesting. I was enjoying it! Other books quickly followed. I met some fellow writers who disagreed with the accepted stories of the time, such as Philo and Josephus. I was amazed to learn that people had been wondering and puzzling over God at least 15,000 years before Moses ever appeared on the scene. Speaking of Moses, I was startled to discover that a group of respected 19th century German biblical scholars had demonstrated through textual research that four smart men, not God (certainly not Moses since he was already dead before the story played out) actually wrote the first five books of the Old Testament—the Torah, or as it's sometimes called, the Pentateuch.

It was both exciting and yet puzzling to discover that next to nothing was known today about Jesus's life then, and nothing written about him until some 40 years after his death. And that Christianity, as a formal religion, didn't actually appear until 300 years after Jesus died—and that because an illiterate emperor named Constantine was urged by his spin-doctors to legitimize the church. It became clear to them that these people called Christians were growing in influence and number—not to mention that with the growing threat from the north, Rome was going to need all the help it could get.

This was all news to me, and I drank it in like free beer. I went through two dozen books on early biblical history, religious thought, the lives of great religious leaders and how religions compete for adherents. I read books that tried to prove God existed and others that tried to prove God didn't exist. During the same time, I began talking to a lot of people about my learning experience. I hadn't shown this much interest in non-technical literature since the advent of *Playboy* in the 60's.

More answers lead to more questions

The education of a rationalist.

I guess that's the right term for a left brainer. Now, almost without being aware of it, I found I was questioning everything about God that I had always taken for granted. Was there really a God? Did God really create the world? Could we see God? Could God hear our prayers? Was God mostly myth and if so, how could something so mystical gather such a world following? Why did God sanction evil in the world? Did God cause the great natural disasters? (One major cable channel did a series on this subject called "The Wrath of God.") Why did so many believe literally and yet so few people question religious orthodoxy? Can you be a moral person and deny God's existence?

The questions kept on coming. How does God relate to man? Who conceived of God in the first place? Then there's the issue of God's future in the world. Was this the result of writers who knew how to tweak my intellectual curiosity? Or was it that having come to the theological well late in life, my thirst was without end? As I grappled with these issues, I found myself wondering if my friends and others dealt with questions like these.

And if not, why not? Were they fessin' up with their real feelings about God? When they sat in church or mosque or temple or synagogue, the words passing over their lips, were they harboring some measure of doubt or indifference? All I knew was that I needed to find answers to the questions.

Conversations about God

Getting personal held the key

Ironically, as I shared my own personal revelations with an ever-widening and diverse group of respondents, the conversations grew more and more enjoyable. I had known some of these people for years, and we had talked about everything and everyone except God. Others were new acquaintances who provided me with intelligent, thoughtful, non-judgmental views and experiences. Thus, for the next two years or so, the stream of dialogue kept flowing—and my mind kept processing the input The first thing I discovered was that searching for the truth about God was a totally different matter from searching for academic or scientific or statistical truth. In this kind of literature, there was speculation galore, leaps of intuitive judgment and suggested scenarios that flared up like bon fires. We are not talking about the history, say, of the fall of the Roman Empire which is carefully documented. God's history is scripted, crafted and…well, woven, much like Joseph's coat of many colors.

DER

To resume...as these conversations grew in number and depth, I started "keeping score." With a growing diversity of my discussion partners, I thought it best to capture the answers in an organized way. Accordingly, I developed a small set of standard "questions" that I managed to work into the conversations. For me to have done any less would have been totally out of character for Dick Levin, statistician. Of course, this process wasn't what you'd call statistically significant sampling. (You would never use words like that in public, would you? I certainly hope not.)

Here are a few of the questions: "Do you often find yourself daydreaming during the worship service?" Next—"does the daydreaming occur more frequently during the sermon or the liturgy?" And finally—"while you're engaged in this parallel activity, are you concerned with whether the God in the liturgy is a God that seems to fit who you are, where you are in your life and what you really believe?" I assume you read sitting down so I can now give you the answers. Just over a third of the participants answered yes to all 3! So what is this telling us? It's telling us that about one out of three of my "discussion partners" spends time during the liturgical part of the service questioning whether the God that is being talked about fits who he is as a person. In the vernacular of an earlier time, that is heavy. Very heavy.

You might be wondering—who are these people? Middle class to upper middle class professionals. About two thirds male, almost all college graduates, a fifth with graduate degrees, and more than three quarters of them actively involved in a religious group. Hardly a representative sample of the American population, but I don't offer this as anything more than what we formal statisticians love to call anecdotal. Now that doesn't mean funny. It just means I wouldn't submit this study for publication in an academic journal—heaven forbid. No, what I've told you are just the mutterings and musings of an engineer/pilot whose flight plan is undergoing some changes—while he's in the air. As an aside and to raise the stakes slightly, study after study indicates that personal accomplishments and emotional fulfillment matter more to regular church or mosque or temple or synagogue attendees than intimacy with your God. Hmmm....

Just where is all this taking us?

Statisticians can go out for strolls, too

Maybe that's what all this is: A walk in the woods. A stroll in the park. I didn't have a goal in sight when it started. I wasn't out to prove or disprove anything. I was just...curious. Anyhow, since I'm off the professional, academic clock, I decided to use these informal findings as a snapshot of how people think about God. Summing up: two thirds are committed to the God that is an integral part of the liturgy, and one third conceptualize other Gods that may be more appropriate for them—or that they're more comfortable with. I may be off a little in my numbers, but hey, I believe a real God loves—and therefore forgives—us statisticians just as much as he does anybody else.

Before I go any further, you need to know that I am a member of the one third I keep talking about. Now comes the question: If you and or I keep day dreaming about the various images of God that do not gel with the tenets or doctrines of our religion, why do we keep on coming to services? Let's go to the findings: the two thirds who don't day dream in parallel reveal the following: they attend (1) to be in God's presence, (2) to feel God's effect, (3) to honor God, (4) to ask God questions and get answers, (5) to learn from God, and (6) to learn from God's behavior. I'm not sure what all of this means—I'm not even sure that they're sure, but there it is.

Okay, what about the one third? Why do they attend? For starters, it's a comforting tradition with interesting rituals that we learn as a child and therefore requires no homework on preparation. In other words, these are habits we acquired early on; if you have kids who need to start out with something religious to believe in, it's hypocritical to ask them to go if you stay home. Some parents drop them off as people used to do their clothes at one-hour martinizing. (Remember that—with their promise of clean as a wink in just one hour?) It worked well with spots and stains on our clothes but not on the soiled or torn fabric of our lives. At least, not in one visit.

So, it's comfortable. It's pleasant. It's convivial. People get to visit with acquaintances they've been too busy to see during the workweek. To chat or schmooze. One can meet new people, make friends, and get acclimated to a new community. It may even serve as an informal job fair, and make no mistake, business is discussed and deals are hatched, if not in fact, certainly the foundations are laid with a nod, a handshake and a luncheon date.

But—if you're a member of the one third, what then? Is it "right" to sit there under what in God's eyes might be false pretenses? Or are you shopping around for the "best deal in town?" Just looking? Hoping and waiting that something may happen.

Is it all right to be moral, join a group, make the world a better place and help others, all the while leaving out the "God part?" If you stood up next Friday or Sunday and proclaimed this was your intent, a lot of folks in those pews would be extremely nervous. Odds are (and that's my business) about two thirds of them would think you had gone off your nut, and would let you know about it through looks that would crack concrete. The real issue, though, is how God would accept a bona fide golden ruler who was a "non-believer." I guess that depends on who or what God we are talking about, doesn't it?

Restating our objectives

Making sure we're on the same page

I said it at the outset and as simply as I could: this is a book about searching for a God that fits you. And just as there are those who buy Ford trucks and those who buy Chevy trucks, there are those who wouldn't be caught dead (bad analogy) speeding in either. Students in seminaries hear lectures about "church shoppers" and how to deal with them. Fact: ruins unearthed from the first century in the holy land have identified the remnants of a Roman temple, a synagogue and a Christian church all on the same street.

The market dynamics reveal an almost unlimited number of choices with constantly rising expectations on the part of consumers. So many choices—what to do? What music do you like? How about sermons, content and style of preaching? Activities, a pastoral rabbi or imam or priest or preacher who likes to visit or one who is prophetic and enjoys "stepping on toes." Frills and baked cookies or fire and brimstone. Gender, color, age, voice, funny, not funny, tall, robed or not robed, open shirt or three button suit with neat tie. Does he or she stand behind the pulpit or come down the aisle? Does the service end in time for you to get a good seat at your favorite Sunday eating place?

It's easy to see that when it comes to choosing a God that "fits you," one size never fits all. But in choosing the meeting place of worship—"God's house," though scriptures clearly downplayed the role of this—one size *can* fit all, though that's not without problems. I have a friend who tells me once he saw a couple new to a church enter on Sunday morning and take their seats, only to be told by an usher that "Uh, you're sitting in the Bagwell's place." (Not their real name.) So now it's come down to reserved spaces in God's parking lot.

Another friend refers to religious groups as "clubs." It turns out there are about 15 million religious congregations on earth today that are divided up into about 500 "master clubs." A lot of them have spent a great deal of money bashing each other, and some of the master clubs have spent millions, often advertising to get people to "switch brands." A sign reads: "The Church Where People Come First." Which begs the question, where exactly do people come at *other* churches? Club bashing can be subtle or brutal, and in the long view of history, it can prove fatal. Understand, these are not questions you have to answer or issues you have to resolve right now. This is not a quiz. No proctors are looking over your shoulder—at least, none of mine. It's an open-ended dialogue written to generate some thinking on your part. No alarm is going to go off signaling it's time to turn over your papers. So relax and kick back. "Yeah, Dick, it's easy for you to do that, you've already made up your mind." That's just it—I haven't.

Making a covenant

Reader and writer

If you belong to the one third who are searchers, "God seekers," I hope I can strengthen your feeling that it's not only O.K. to search but good for you as well. I'll try diligently to provide you with relevant information and useful suggestions that my experience indicates have worked for others—and for me. Moreover, I hope that these will make your search more effective and rewarding. That's for the one third. For the two-thirds who say they are comfortable with their God and not looking, I commend you for your tolerance of the rest of us. And I envy you in your comfort zone.

What's in this book for Dick?

Ah-hah, now we get to the good part.

Actually, prior to writing Chapter One, I've already grown from my reading, the research and the conversations. Nonetheless, I am aware that I am starting out on a journey that, even though I have an outline, I will encounter unknowns along the way like huge boulders on a moonless night; and without first walking around them, I can't plot their mass or dimensions in advance. Boy, that's humbling for an engineer. And right now, I'm about as humble as I can stand about how little I still know about the subject of God even after all this work. My sense of God, however, has been given a thorough vetting, up, down and sideways and hung out wet on the line to dry in the bright sun of reason and hope.

Specifically, what have I learned? A great deal about how people think about God. How they search for a conceptualization of God that fits them better. And finally, how they go about making that choice. Additionally, I have met those who suffer frustration and disbelief and pain about their God, but who for reasons known only to them—reasons that perhaps they never admit to themselves except in the dark of night when the moon casts no shadow and their heart beats like a drum—never alter their concept of God. Either it's too late, it's too hard, I owe God this, I can't back out, I don't want to make him angry...and what if I did, what might happen to me? If only I could _____. You fill in the blank.

Remember the children of Israel saying to Moses, "If only we had stayed in Egypt". If only.... If they had, the history of the world—and therefore of God—would have been changed forever. In the place where I am now, I think that God is not a God of "if only" but rather of "why not!" And on that thought, this is a good point to take a breather, stretch, sip some coffee or water, then come back for what I hope will be an exciting exploration of discovery and revelation—the History of God, Parts I and II. Remember, nobody is running a clock on you. But you say, "Dick, there are only 24 hours in the day." My answer to that was best captured by a wonderful Spanish philosopher, Jose Ortega y Gasset who said, "life is fired at us point blank." And at this moment, our sights are set on God's history, as recorded by our fellow right and left brainers. The unedited script is 40,000 years long, but I hope we can cover it in record time. So get comfortable...and enjoy the trip!

CHAPTER 2

A BRIEF HISTORY OF
GOD (PART 1)

The Ancients and their take on God. Or god.

S mall "g," big "G," it was all the same to them, since they knew or at least, believed that somebody up there either liked—or didn't like them. Life's like that, then and now. Tough, short and fragile. They just couldn't find the right place to stick a pin on the cosmic map.

But then, human beings have always imagined, created, worshipped (and sometimes destroyed) Gods. Similarly, theologians, proper and otherwise, have always disagreed about when, why, where and in what form the God business all began; but one thing they do agree on is that God-creating, as well as God-bashing, has always been popular. It's my guess that early cave paintings were probably more an attempt to express wonderment, than they were an explanation of natural phenomena. Put another way, somebody woke up at three in the morning, had an itch and while the fire still glowed, scratched his musings on a rock wall, then went back to bed.

After the Paleolithic Period that ended about 40,000 years ago, the worship of the Mother Goddess became focused on the one thing that kept everybody's stomach from growling. Agriculture. Bottom line—the none-too-deep furrow they plowed with a stick morphed into Wall Street—a bad trade off but it's all the same. Humans like to see things grow, whether it's barley or bonuses. The important thing is: archeologists and others crazy enough to dig in a hot sun for fame and blisters, found carved statues of the Mother Goddess over a wide area of Europe. Early one morning, somebody probably stood on a rock and shouted, "It's the land, stupid," and the people grunted their assent.

Everything good came out of the soil, and that was because the right stuff that fell from the sky (sun, rain and the like) completed the right side of the equation. What good was land without water? What good did it do to plant seeds if the sun didn't shine? And when the good stuff came down, the conventional wisdom was, as we said in the beginning, "somebody up there likes us." And when it *didn't* happen...that marked history's first theological debate.

Deity modeling and make-overs

Men and their earliest gods

In the Middle East about 50 centuries ago, people started to believe that by imitating the gods, they might share in their power and immortality. What happened in the gods' world was a model for everything here on earth. In ancient Persia, for example, every real thing had its spiritual counterpart in the "sacred" world.

Before we go any further, a word about historical dating. What used to be designated as BC, *Before Christ*, is now referred to by many as BCE, *Before the Common Era*. Similarly, AD from the Latin, *Anno Domini—the year of the Lord*—became CE—the Common Era. Ap-

parently, some theologians felt that neutral, non-religious terms would be less offensive to the non-Christian majority in the world. If you've ever wondered about this, now you know. And if you haven't, then pardon the academic detour. One additional note: as surprising as it may seem, the change generated almost as much furor as was created about other seemingly far more controversial topics such as homosexuality and abortion. Indeed, the Southern Baptist Convention, meeting in 2000 in Orlando, released a statement that read in part, "...the [BCE/CE method] is the result of the secularization, anti-supernaturalism, religious pluralism and political correctness pervasive in our society," and further, urged all SBC individuals and churches to avoid this "revisionism." And now, back to our story.

About 4000 BCE, in what is now Iraq, the Sumerians developed a written language—a must in order to keep up with agricultural accounts. How many bags of grain did A sell to B? This in turn gave rise to laws, literature and mythology. Temples sprang up. Now, let's fast forward to 2000 BCE when the Amorites wanted a larger slice of the agricultural pie, invaded the land and made Babylon the capital. Later, in 800 BCE—50 years after the founding of Rome—Babylon was captured by the Assyrians, and the Babylonian culture spread like a wave over Canaan, the ancient "promised land" of the Israelites. Hewing to the conventional wisdom, the Babylonians believed that the gods were the source of their power and conquests, and to show their gratitude, they attempted to remake Babylon into the gods' home or their earthbound version of heaven. Ten days a year, the Babylonians celebrated a New Year festival including a recitation of their epic poem, *Enuma Elish,* a celebration of the gods' triumph over chaos. Questions about the origins of life were put aside: after all, no one had been there at creation so who knew? The great poem was steeped in mystery, and they hoped the symbolism would give them power. In this early expression of spirituality lay hints of the monotheism that was yet to come.

The Babylonians' take on creation was that their gods rose out of a watery waste—ancient wizards of ooze. It resembled the swamps of Mesopotamia where floods were a constant danger. And the gods? They quarreled, fought, had kids, griped about their perks, separated sky from earth, built a temple and then outdid themselves—or maybe they were just lonely. And in the process, they created humans. The first man was made from that same muck; hence human and gods—divinity and humanity—were opposite sides of the same coin.

Meanwhile, in nearby Canaan, which would later become Israel, the Canaanites put their unique spin on all this. They already had their own set of gods including the god of fertility and storms, Baal-Habad (who is mentioned in the Bible). Not surprisingly, Baal fought other gods; they built him a palace; he slew a seven-headed dragon, died and was even brought back to life—a recurring theme of ancient theology. Interestingly, the Canaanites practiced ritual sex with priestesses. They thought that by copying the gods' behavior—blending the art of the practical with the aesthetics of pleasure—they would avoid sterility and people the earth. I ask you—how clever can you be?

Origin of the one God of the Jews

Abram takes a trip

In Genesis, Chapter 12, the writer tells us that Abram received traveling orders from a god called Yahweh and trekked from Mesopotamia ("between the rivers") to the Mediterranean Sea. This was a bold shift from the earlier Babylonian gods who didn't meddle in the everyday lives of their worshippers. Now they had a god who was the author of real change in the real world—a god who wanted to play an active role in the here and now.

Abraham spoke a Semitic (from Noah's son, Shem) language called Hebrew and was certainly no saint. Rather, he is described as a mercenary, a trade that paid well enough and signaled rival tribes to give you a wide berth. More important, he practiced the religion we have been describing and from time to time would even have "conversations" with Yahweh.

According to Genesis, three waves of early Hebrews settled in Canaan. Abraham in 1850; Jacob (his grandson) in what is now Nablus and a third wave arriving from Egypt in about 1200, the latter scenario being Hollywood's favorite. This final wave is important primarily because they claimed to have been liberated from Pharaoh by Yahweh—meaning, the Lord of Hosts which in our terms would be a five star general with divine ambitions. This God of Moses was the very same who spoke to Abram, renaming him Abraham, the "Father of Nations." The same whose spirit or *Ruach* would fill the rabbi named Yeshua. This God who eighteen centuries later would sweep up Mohammed in a fierce hug in one life-changing moment. Thus, a personal relationship between man and God was well underway. Conclusion: the story of their exodus from Egypt was central to their emerging identity, and after being kept alive by being retold around campfires, it was finally put in writing about four centuries after their arrival in Canaan.

A brief word about the Bible

Will the real author please stand up?

About two centuries ago, German biblical scholars set forth an astounding theory. It wasn't Moses who wrote the first five books of the Bible, as had commonly been held, but rather four different people (maybe *groups* of people) who wrote the Pentateuch: Genesis, Exodus, Leviticus, Numbers and Deuteronomy —finally codified into the Torah by about 500 BCE. This helps to explain the different treatments of the same events (i.e., the two accounts of how and why the Israelites left Egypt). Briefly: the scholars identified one writer as "J" because he called God Yahweh; the other writer "E" called his God Elohim. There'll be more about the other two, "D" and "P," a bit later.

Consider: the earliest gods had kept their distance from humans. The younger Babylonian gods started to mix in with ordinary affairs, but now here was Yahweh who produced *miracles!* He saved Moses and his people. Here's a little *did you know?* The Sea of Reeds the Israelites crossed was mistakenly identified as the Red Sea and still is to this day. In exchange for Yahweh's involving himself in the lives of the "children of Israel," God now drew a line between himself and man. For when Moses reached Mount Sinai, he warned his people not to climb the mountain or even touch it under pain of death. This may have been the first recorded mother of all lines in the sand. While Moses scaled the heights, his people stewed and fretted, their faith fading into the desert sunset. Finally, they made a golden bull and worshipped it just as they had back in Canaan. Monotheism was okay, but if you were smart, you covered all the bases.

The Axial Age

Currents east and west

In the period 800-200, BCE, lots of new religious structures and ideologies were conceived. But the real focus of the people was on commerce, and a newly emerging merchant class became ever more powerful in the control of daily life.

Halfway into the Age, the famed Greek philosopher Socrates said "religion is not good because the gods approve of it but the gods *approve* of it because it *is* good." People pondered this for a while, and you may do the same. It's just one of many seminal thoughts, revelations and observations that I come across, broadcast like seed in a freshly-plowed field, waiting to sprout.

As I walk this field, the feel of the earth underfoot, the smell of the loam and the rise and slope of ancient furrows form a kind of sensory mosaic. Something is happening. Studying God—even for a confirmed engineer/rationalist like me—cannot help but have its effect upon one; and though I am a harder sell than most, I am neither deaf nor blind to the experience.

A thousand years earlier, people from what is now Iran invaded what is now India and imposed their religious ideas contained in their *Rig-Veda.* At the core of these was a multitude of gods much like the deities of the Middle East—plus a belief that their myths were not descriptions of reality but rather mysteries which even the gods had trouble explaining. The believers (Vedas) didn't debate the origins of life, but helped people come to grips with the vicissitudes of daily living and still remain reverent toward the gods.

But by the start of the Axial Age, the Vedic religion faded in favor of Karma—the notion that destiny is the product of one's actions. Vedics had been caught up in sacrifices, now supplanted by Yoga which focused mental power through intense concentration. Just in time for those East Indians who, now tired of sacrifices, searched for the inner meanings of what they had been practicing. A sea change followed: Gods became unimportant, replaced by religious teachers. Rather than deny the existence of gods, however, the two new religions, Hinduism and its offspring, Buddhism, tried to find ways to go *beyond* gods.

The holy power in Vedic came from sacrifice and was called Brahman. This entity neither "talks" to us nor is a supreme deity. Its purpose is to inspire and sustain us. Like a work of fine art, Brahman is what "cannot be spoken in words" nor can it be explained rationally. Clearly, one must be intelligent to create that work of art, but Brahman goes beyond intelligence. This constitutes another major shift from earlier thinking which we'll have more to say about later.

Philosophers, Mystics and Prophets

At about the same time the Jews left Babylon and began rebuilding the Temple, (538 BCE) an Indian ascetic, Gautama, left his wife, child and home and for six years, sat at the feet of Hindu gurus to learn how to rid the world of its pain. One day in a trance, he gained enlightenment and became the Buddha. (A whole generation of modern-day minor gurus have emerged as self-proclaimed seekers of truth. In no way do I denigrate the earnestness of their search, but oftentimes, along with the small statue of Buddha in their room comes a BMW in the garage. The Gautama would not be amused.) Buddha's focus was Dharma—not about God, but rather the truth about how to live. The Buddha didn't argue God's existence: it was just that a non-personal God wasn't of much use to humans. Whereas Karma proposed continuous rebirth, the Buddha saw the end goal as Nirvana, a state analogous to God. In the Judeo-Christian paradigm, this may well approximate "the peace that passes all understanding."

When he was asked if a Buddha who reached Nirvana lived after death, he said the question "was not proper." It should be noted that many Jews, Christians and Muslims give the same reply to questions about the afterlife.

Plato (428-348 BCE) lived his 80 years believing that a soul was a rejected deity, in a tomb—the body. He was greatly influenced by Pythagoras, who some believe was himself influenced by ideas from India. In Plato's view, divine existence transcended our senses: things in our world are only imitations of things in the world of the divine. Aristotle, (384-322) a contemporary, took another tack—through logic you could actually understand the universe. Yet, even with this scientific focus, Aristotle gave credence to religion and mythology. He felt that people who followed a particular religion did not have to learn facts but simply experience emotion and certain dispositions; and this was to have a profound influence on monotheism. He saw reality as a hierarchy of existences, each layer affecting the one below it, though progressively weaker. Interestingly but predictably, Aristotle's God neither created the world nor was its caretaker.

Wrap-up

These Axial Age ideologies all agreed there was a transcendent element in life—one beyond human knowledge and existing apart *from* the material universe. Put another way, there was something unseen that was a vital component of human development. The only problem is they were never clear whether this was (1) simply the old mythologies repackaged or (2) an entirely new concept. That decision was to come much later.

It may be a bit early in the game for a seventh inning stretch, but we're going to take one anyway. Some of you may be asking yourself: does all this information really matter? And some not so patient may even be thinking of reaching for the remote. Not a good move and here's why. God—your choice, your version—has spent thousands of years getting us to this point, and our putting the pieces of the puzzle together is hard work, but, I promise you, it'll be worth it. The people we're telling you about are the major players in what is the world's longest running series. Granted, at the very best, we can give you only a snapshot of most of them, but we hope these images will stay fairly fresh in your mind. If not, there's always the reader's option of thumbing back to look somebody up. In any event, we invite you to stay tuned, with the promise that the rewards will more than justify the effort. Thanks.

The transition to one God

Too many deities ruin the blessing.

It's the 7th century BCE in Judea, the southern kingdom. Things are definitely not good. The people hadn't given up on Yahweh, but they weren't going to let go of their pagan gods either. To the north, the Assyrians were licking their chops over the prospects of conquest; the 10 tribes of Northern Israel were assimilated and disappeared; and in 10 years, half as many kings had come and gone. In short, a mess.

Enter Isaiah, a member of Judea' s ruling family. Destined to become Israel's major prophet, he feared for the future of his people. One day while praying in one of King Solomon's temples about his own spiritual shortcomings, he suddenly faced Yahweh who designated Isaiah as his messenger—and the news he was given to deliver was not good. In less than 40 years, Judea would suffer invasion, destruction of its cities, deportation of citizens and imprisonment of the Jewish king in Jerusalem. Isaiah was brought to his knees. Yahweh had already shown himself to be a major player putting new hinges on the door of history. His competition was a rag tag team of bush leaguers who dabbled in mythology. And now here comes Yahweh, forecasting defeat and bringing sorrow.

Worse yet, he deplored animal sacrifices in the temple, calling them useless and an "abomination." It was time, he told the trembling Isaiah, for the Israelites to discover what religion really meant. In a word, this God of Isaiah, insisted on meaning, not sacrifice. Isaiah's message was lent additional thrust by Amos and Hosea, two contemporaries who sounded a similar warning and the threat of impending doom.

With this in-your-face language fired at them point blank, you would have thought Yahweh could have persuaded his people to give the lesser gods the bum's rush. But progress was slow and difficult. Finally, toward the end of the 7th century BCE, Josiah, the King of Judah, made his move. People can no longer worship the old Canaan gods while worshipping Yahweh. The story goes that the priest Hilkiah comes across a very old account of Moses' last sermon to the Israelites illustrating the seeming indifference to Yahweh's earliest instructions to the grand old leader. And now, a surprise! There is evidence that this discovery was an early version of the book of Deuteronomy (remember "D" the writer we told you about?). Well, the new version contained the ancient profession of Jewish faith, the hallowed *Shema* calling the Jews to worship: "Hear, oh Israel...." The language includes the words "God is one" which on its face suggests monotheism was already grounded in reality and practice.

But in fact, the people, fickle as ever, were still hanging out with other attractive gods. Thus, what the prayer *did* mean was simply this: "Yes, you have lots of choices in the marketplace, but I, Yahweh, am the only true God, and you are permitted to worship no other." Clearly, Yahweh's reputation as a jealous God had not been diminished. The two kings before Josiah had all but ignored these kinds of warnings, but Josiah, terrified of what God might do—tearing his children from the womb of the land and scattering them like seed—ordered that all god symbols be destroyed. Moreover, biblical scholars assert that the ensuing destruction actually came from the fear and anxiety caused by God's words that exploded with righteous force.

As though Isaiah hadn't gotten the message across, Jeremiah strode upon the scene near the end of the 6th century BCE. He was known as the "weeping prophet" because of his great empathy for Israel. (They may not always kill the messenger, as happened to Isaiah, but they can make his life a hell on earth, and so it was with Jeremiah.) Nonetheless, following God's orders, he chastised his people, while things were going from bad to worse. The Babylonians invaded Israel, the King was taken into exile and Jerusalem was surrounded. Moaning and wailing filled the air; chaos and fear gripped the populace. Jerusalem fell and then came the ultimate horror—the temple was destroyed. Yet, Jeremiah saw in all of this a new hope: these things had been only symbols. True belief in God could not be etched in stone and mortar, but had to be written on people's hearts.

Ezekiel and his chariot

A vision on wheels

He had been a street preacher in Babylon with only a small following. But when King Cyrus conquered Nebuchadnezzar and gave the Jews their freedom (along with enough money to rebuild the temple) Ezekiel returned to his homeland and stayed alone in his house in Tel Aviv for five years. Then came the vision: Ezekiel saw a chariot with flashing lights, being pulled by four different animals each with four different heads, but what was strangest—the wheels revolved in different directions. What was going on here? Was our fearless prophet on something?

No, he was on *to* something! Ezekiel saw the wheels as symbols of the inherent dissonance in the vision of God he was commanded to teach the people. And along with teaching, he was ordered to do a number of other things (including eating excrement)—graphic proof of how different—not to mention difficult and demanding—Yahweh's religion was from that of the pagans. Ezekiel was making his point that Israel's history and its attendant miseries weren't just random occurrences. I can hear him now—*listen up, people!*

The one God who speaks with one voice

The problem is: what does it all mean?

For those of you keeping textual score, the first distinct Old Testament reference to one God is found in Isaiah 45:2 1. "No God was formed before me nor will be after me. I am Yahweh, there is no savior but me." Now, nothing is known about who wrote this, but it was thrown in with Isaiah, and its author is referred to as Second Isaiah. It's also the first time the

Israelites focus on God's role in creation, for the conventional wisdom went thus: if God had triumphed in primordial times, surely he could save them now when they were in perilous circumstances. After all, hadn't he just told them that he was the one and only God?

But Yahweh, the one God, was not easily understood. Isaiah 55:8-9 says, "My thoughts are not your thoughts. My ways are not your ways, it is Yahweh who speaks. Yes, the heavens are as high above earth as my ways above your ways, my thoughts above your thoughts." The one God was beyond people, he was beyond words, and he would not always do what people wanted. In divine shorthand, "I don't have to explain myself to you...so don't ask." This was hard for the Israelites to swallow, as indeed, it is for us today. Therein lies part of the dilemma and challenge of each of us finding a God that fits.

Remember, we were looking for writers and had found two. The third has now surfaced: the priestly writer, designated as "P." Credited with authoring *Leviticus* and *Numbers,* "P" has a much more exalted view of God and unlike "J," didn't believe God could be seen. "P's" best known contribution to the Bible, however was the story of creation in Genesis. In the Babylonian *Enuma Elish,* there were 6 days for creation and then a day of rest. In *Deuteronomy,* the 7th day was a day of rest for everybody, even the slaves. But "P" has a different take on things: the Sabbath should be a day to imitate God's behavior and reflect on the creation itself. A boat builder stepping back and admiring his craftsmanship. Will it sail? Will it sink? Will it skim over the waves or founder in the swells? We would say, it depends largely upon who is at the wheel.

Beware of Greeks bearing thoughts

With the Romans not far behind

Philosophy was the Greek's stock in trade in the 4th century BCE, energized by the fact that a century earlier, 17 consonants and 7 vowels came trooping in all in a row. The alphabet had arrived! Writing and reading became favorite pastimes, and as the fingers scrawled and the mind grew, Greek ideas and culture spread like a river overflowing its banks, all the way to Israel. Greek sports, art and philosophy were a refreshing surprise to the "people of the book." Some Jews took Greek names and fought in their army. And some Greeks came to know (and even worship) Yahweh in these strange new synagogues (Greek for "meeting places") that did not offer sacrifices. But most Greeks and Jews stuck with their beliefs, and this refusal of the Jews to acknowledge that Greek gods even existed led to them being called atheists.

Jews continued to hold that wisdom was fear of God and not related to Greek rationalism. The author(s) of the Book of Proverbs in the 3rd century BCE, even suggested that wisdom was God's plan for humanity. In *The Wisdom of Solomon,* 200 years later, an Egyptian Jew echoed Proverbs and counseled Jews to resist the attractions of Greek culture and remember: wisdom is fear of Yahweh. This writer knew that the Greek gods were a product of rational thinking, implying that thinking humans were close to the gods. The difference with Yahweh was that he only revealed himself to his prophets, and then only when it suited his purpose.

In Alexandria, a city of great learning and culture, lived the eminent and devout Jewish philosopher, Philo (30 BCE —45 CE). Philo could see no reason why the attractive, monotheistic God of the Jews could not be merged with the rational Greek god. In order to do this, he had one hurdle to clear: how the Greek gods (lacking human physiology) could comport with Yahweh who revealed himself to prophets. Philo devised a neat philosophical trick (thereby assuring his place in history) by dividing God's behavior into two parts (1) the essence of God which no human can know anything about, and (2) God's power which is quite evident to us mere mortals. Historically, Jews have rejected this model. At Philo's death, the relationship between the Jews and Greeks collapsed, eventually leading to attacks against the million or so Jews who lived in Alexandria.

Then, as now, land and religion remained the two possessions men were most determined to fight over—and die for.

After the death of Alexander (323 BCE) gradually the Roman Empire began to spread into Africa and the Middle East. Originally, the Romans had no animosity toward the Jews. Admittedly, a bit strange in their habits, the Jews tended their shops and flocks, paid their taxes and though fond of arguing, were ideal citizens. Business was good. But in the year 66 CE, a group of political zealots organized a rebellion (the 1st Jewish-Roman war) and were brutally crushed. In 70, Jerusalem was captured and the temple destroyed again.

Earlier in the century, new religious sects had been formed—the Essenes and Pharisees among them—and some of these weren't all that sad to see the temple go. Corruption had been growing within the system, and anyway, God did not need a fortress-like mansion on a hill with an altar drenched in animal blood and belching smoke. (Hadn't Isaiah told them that?) Rather, he made himself known in the simplest activities of the daily round. The rabbis noted this shift and gladly obliged.

BEWARE OF GREEKS BEARING THOUGHTS

YAHWEH

GREEK GODS

DER

Not wanting to hold the leash too tightly on their new subjects, the Romans allowed the Pharisees to form a community near Jerusalem under Rabbi Yohannan. The Rabbi was a champion of acts of loving kindness and would quote Yahweh as saying, "I desire mercy and not sacrifice." Other communities sprang up, and together they formed a generation of rabbinic scholars known as *tannaim,* including Yohannan, Rabbi Akiva and Rabbi Ishmael. The last of these brought the law of Moses up to date by writing down the previously oral law, the *Mishnah.* This process of study, meditation and codification became the pragmatic norm for Judaism. After all, it worked, had it not, thus saving an entire people. Central to all the rabbis' teaching was the sanctity of life. (Twenty centuries later at his hospital in Lambarene, Africa, Albert Schweitzer would echo this thought: *erfurcht fur dem Leben,* "a reverence for life.")

The precepts of rabbinic Judaism were grounded in a passionate yet simple logic: because everyone was created in God's image, everyone was equal before God. Jews were taught to create a sense of God *within themselves,* and over the centuries, Yahweh became a force that would positively affect all human encounters.

Jesus and God

Well...is he or isn't he?

More books have been written about Jesus than about any other figure in history; and yet, in terms of reliable facts, we know very little. Fact: he was a charismatic faith healer from the Galilee. Fact: he made his living as a "home repairman" mending, fixing, doing rough carpentry jobs and the like, until the final three years of his life. There are no photographs, no identity kits or composites and no authentic pictorial records from the time. Throughout the ages, great artists would portray him with aquiline features, blue eyes, fair complexion, blond or light brown hair, but in all likelihood, Jesus (Hebrew name:

Yeshua) was a dark skinned, dark-haired, dark-eyed Mediterranean Jew of slight build and average height.

The first written account of Jesus by a writer named John Mark was written over 40 years after Jesus died—hardly more than a verbal snapshot. As memories faded during those 40 years, myths sprouted like desert flowers on the Gallilean hillsides. Historians and hyperbole are no stranger to one another—witness the devotees of George Washington and their tales about the cherry tree, throwing a dollar across the Potomac and the like. In truth, many scholars regard this refurbishing of the birth and life narrative of Jesus as a natural expression of the passionate devotion of Jesus' followers.

Because it was the most current, Mark is thought to be the most reliable of the gospels. Mark sees Jesus as a very normal person—the son of a carpenter who became a teacher (rabbi). Mark also describes Jesus' mentor, John, as a wandering, admittedly "far out" member of the Essenes whose home base was at the Qumran community. The latter sect believed that Jerusalem was hopelessly corrupt; thus, John urged his listeners to adopt the Essene right of purification in the River Jordan. Jesus gladly complied, and as he emerged, Mark wrote that the "heavens were torn apart, and a voice from heaven said, 'you are my son, the Beloved.'" Actually, this event was not all that unusual, many rabbis reporting similar experiences following this ritual immersion.

History records there were many faith healers like Jesus roaming the countryside. They also taught, healed the sick and even exorcised demons. Some scholars claim that, like Paul, Jesus was a Pharisee. (The word has received bad press over the years, but it originally meant "holy purist.") In any event, after Jesus died and after due deliberation, his followers decided he had been more than just another man. They did not think he was God in human form, at least, not then. (That idea didn't take root for another 300 years). Nor is there any evidence that Jesus *claimed* he was God. The Gospels report that God gave Jesus divine powers, but then Jesus believed that his disciples could exercise the same powers if they had faith—which he defined as surrender of the self to God.

His disciples prayed *to* him for some time, but Paul never called Jesus "God." He did refer to him as the son of God but only in the Jewish sense of a person who lives by God's dictums. (One of the earliest referrals to son-ship occurs in Exodus 4:22, God says to Pharoah, "Israel is my first born son.") Paul did believe, however, that Jesus had supplanted the Torah as God's principal revealer, and further, that Jesus had been the Messiah. The tentmaker turned evangelist maintained that Jesus had achieved things that the Israel of his time had not been able to bring about—moreover, that he represented an entirely new type of society from which no one was excluded. It was at this time that Paul introduced the name "Christ"—in Hebrew, *Moschiach...* "the anointed one."

Clearly, the idea of incarnating God *in* a human—in this instance, Jesus—was an oft-recurring idea in religious history, most particularly in Buddhism and Hinduism. Having said that, the very idea was anathema to Paul as a Jew. Centuries later, it would become so to Muslims as well.

The early church gets off the ground

Divisions, debates and otherwise

For the first 70 years after Jesus died, his followers (first called Messianists, then Christians by the year 47) prayed to Jesus as Jews. The Romans considered these people just one more sect of Judaism, but when they announced they were not, the Romans saw them as lacking piety or having broken the faith, and this did not sit well with the Emperor. In Rome, you always followed the party line.

A baker's dozen of other issues arose during this time, and we'll mention just one. An Egyptian convert to Christianity named Clement, believed that Jesus *was* God. But in so doing, he created a dilemma. How could Jesus be considered divine and the people still worship one God? This was a real puzzler.

In Rome at about the same time, a little known figure, Sabellius, suggested an answer: the one God of the Jews wore three different masks at different times: father, son and holy spirit. Although this idea would get traction in the future, now it was soundly rejected. The Bishop of Antioch tried another approach—Jesus was just another man in whom God's wisdom dwelt. Also rejected. Finally, Clement's pupil, Origen suggested that the virgin birth of Jesus was not to be thought of as an actual physical event but rather the birth of divine wisdom; further, believing that Jesus was divine was only a temporary step until we actually met God. The Romans not only pooh-poohed Origen's little gem, they condemned it as heresy. (Origen was, to be kind, a bit strange.)

Wrap-up

As Christianity became increasingly important in this part of the world—indeed, Rome was finding it more and more difficult to ignore its presence—the religious leaders and followers of the day struggled with how Jesus as a divine person could coexist with their strongly felt belief in one God.

Two different Gods

Or just one more debate

The early fourth century (CE) saw Christian leaders and their followers focused on the relationship between God the father and God the son (Jesus). Jesus had, of course, clearly stated that God was greater, but that didn't help resolve the theological brouhaha. An Egyptian Christian, Arius, kicked off the argument by asking his bishop, "how could Christ have been God like God the father is God?" From there, things heated up, and the emperor Constantine, who had no interest in or knowledge of theology, organized a conference in Turkey. *We'll settle this thing once and for all.*

Both sides were represented: Arius on the one hand and Athanasius (the Bishop Alexander's sidekick) on the other.

Athanasius had no doubt that Jesus was a God, too; and when the vote was taken, Athanasius won, but not unanimously. The result was the Nicene Creed which exists in many forms, one of which begins thusly: "I believe in one God the Father Almighty, maker of all things, visible and invisible and in one Lord, Jesus Christ, the Son of God, the only begotten of the Father, that is of the substance of the Father...."

Those attending breathed a sigh of relief, and Constantine patted himself on the back. The only problem was: after the meeting, things went on exactly as before. The bishops never budged from their position, and the Arius-Athanasius debate kept smoldering for at least another half century. To say Christians were confused is a gross understatement. In desperation (or perhaps inspiration) three practitioners of the Eastern Orthodox Church in Cappadocia, Turkey, came up with an idea they thought might work. The three were well-versed in Greek rational discourse, but also recognized the role of mythology in teaching—albeit it could not be demonstrated scientifically. The three theologians proposed a dictum that said public teaching about the church should come directly and solely from the Bible. On the other hand, *dogma* (as they referred to it) was the deeper symbolic meaning of what had been written and could only be comprehended through religious experience. Moreover, they actually thought of this dogma as secret, and believed that the uninitiated were not allowed to see these ideas; therefore, they should not be written down. (Is everybody clear on this?)

Strange as it may seem, later on, Jews and Muslims adopted this idea, i.e. that some of what was true in religion (um—the secret part) could not be defined or expressed logically. If you'll recall, the Buddha had already noted that some questions about God were improper and could not be answered with words; in fact, Galatians 1:11-14 even proposes that these secrets were better suggested by silence. In fairness, biblical scholars don't believe any of this was an attempt to shut lay-people out of religion, but rather an admission (confession?) that some religious truths just could not be expressed logically.

This is a very important concept in the history of God. Gregory of Nyssa, a Greek Orthodox Church leader, summed this up in his book, *Life of Moses*—"we cannot see God intellectually, but if we let ourselves be enveloped in the cloud that descended from Mt. Sinai, we will *feel* (italics mine) his presence." There's only one problem; this still does not answer the question: how can we have multiple Gods in a belief system called monotheism? Something like this could give cognitive dissonance a bad name.

Examining the Trinity

Theology's answer to arm wrestling

Back to those three hapless Cappadocians tussling with the issue of multiple Gods. They tried to shed light on this by declaring that God was a single divine being who, when he shows himself to the world, is three forces: Father, Son and Spirit. So far so good. Gregory of Nyssa went further: to him, the idea that there are three Gods, or that God might actually split himself into three parts, was blasphemous. What Gregory said was that God revealed himself in all these forms—when he wanted the world to see him.

Many Christians in the West still find the concept of a trinity puzzling. Some Sunday school teachers of children tell them it's like water: it can be liquid, ice or steam. (Sounds good to an eight year old, but can it take the heat?) Back to history: Basil, in his Epistle 38:4, warned Christians against trying to figure out how the three outside views of God (hypostases) could be both one and distinctly three. Indeed, many theologians warn against trying to interpret the Trinity literally; and some even believe that the three Cappadocians (they're starting to sound like a comedy act) devised their three forces concept to keep their God different from the rational Greek God of Plato. It has been said by some that the real purpose of the Trinity is to remind humans that they simply *cannot* grasp the reality of God and therefore, should not think of God in human terms.

What's Augustine's take on this? One of the most memorable pillars of Western thought, this was the man who defined the Trinity for the Latin Church. Though his training was razor sharp Greek rationalism, the Bishop of Milan persuaded Augustine that Christianity was fully compatible with the hard-edged rationality of Plato. The Bishop wanted to baptize Augustine, but having admitted in his *Confessions* he was not celibate (and believing his faith required him to be) Augustine demurred. When he was eventually converted and baptized, it was said the event was tumultuous. Regrettably, no cameras were allowed.

Augustine believed that God was not a reality, but a spiritual presence in everyone—further, that God was highly personal. Amazingly, he shared this notion with many others, including Buddhists, Hindus and even leaders of pagan religions. In the 5th century CE, Augustine developed his own rather complex psychological theory of the Trinity. In the soul, he said, one finds memory, understanding and will. Like the Trinity of the Cappadocians, he said that these three parts of the soul represent one life and one mind. The trinity is, in fact, within each of us and is the divine faith in three parts: (1) holding the truths of the Incarnation of Jesus in our minds; (2) contemplating them; and (3) delighting in them. Only in this way can we realize the Trinity and its meaning.

One final thought. (First take a deep breath.) Augustine left us with a curious tidbit of religious history—his own concept of original sin. He said that God had destined mankind to eternal damnation for Adam's one transgression, and that this guilt was passed on from generation to generation in the sexual act, which he saw as a human attempt to take pleasure from women instead of from God. (I did warn you.) Religion that had originally been highly disposed *toward* women, had already started showing misogynistic tendencies before Augustine. There are, for instance, the letters of Jerome, little more than deranged rants, and now we find Augustine puzzled as to why God made women at all. Although contemporary Jews and Greek Orthodox Christians view Augustine's gender barbs with dismay, some religious historians claim that the failure to ordain women may be evidence that Western Christianity has never fully recovered from Augustine. This is the same man who took a mistress (the polite term was *concubine)* at the age of 18 and fathered an illegitimate son at 19. As he put it, "I never passed up an opportunity to pursue one sin or another." Of course, he eventually confessed all this in…where else, his *Confessions.*

The 99 names of God

A desert preacher finds his voice

If I tell you about a man who was born poor, became a merchant, married a rich widow, had one-on-one conversations with the angel, Gabriel, and then became, as he put it, "God's publisher," you might start to wonder about me. This is not helpful to our cause so let's dig further.

For openers, Mohammed is sometimes spelled Muhammad, but that's all right: Jewish Chanukah can be Hanukkah or even Chanukkah.

In any event, Mohammed asserted the Lordship of a God named Allah, which Arabs thought of as being identical to the God of the Christians and the Jews. So far, so good. Except in the case of Mohammed; for his pains he was tagged a sorcerer, a false prophet and was said to be possessed. Not exactly the best press to have if you're a forty-year-old, trying to get a new belief system off the ground.

The problem? Essentially, Mohammed (570-632) was disturbed because the old and revered values of the nomad Bedouins had succumbed to the appetites of local capitalism. Granted, people now had money and were big time traders, but in Mohammed's view this was no way to run a religion. The Arabs worshipped a set of pagan gods at shrines (actually a black stone) but there was no mythical uplink to a spiritual life. What to do?

First things first. While at the annual Ramadan retreat, Mohammed asked God to send a prophet to set his people on the right path. While praying, he felt an angel of God crush him in his arms and command that he begin reciting Holy Scripture. Mohammed did just that, and his utterances would later become the Koran. And for the next 23 years, during trances and periods of unconsciousness, Islam's holy book was given to him piece by piece—not at all like God' s revealing the first five books of the Bible (the Torah) to Moses in one fell swoop on Mount Sinai. Mohammed, not being literate, had to memorize the Koran; and it was only later that people who could write recorded it for history, this finally being completed a generation after his death. Interestingly, Mohammed never had to argue the existence of God. The people already believed that; the real thrust of the text, and it surfaces early on, was a commandment to take a good look around and acknowledge how much they owed God for what he had done. Point being: in the Koran, atheists are not non-believers but rather ungrateful people who owe God but won't admit it. (This thesis would make a book unto itself.)

In trying to understand Islam, let's start at square one—where else but sin. For Islam, it's idolatry. Koran denounces pagan deities, just like the Pentateuch. The divinity is one. And it rejects the idea that God would beget a son. Simply put, God created the world so that we could know him. Further, we see God only in his actions, and the majesty and power of this one God is given voice by the 99 different names he is given in the Koran. (You can look it up.)

Consider: both Jews and Muslims have scratched pork off the menu, and pray three and five times a day respectively toward Jerusalem. (If that sounds a bit much, you should know that nearly all orders of monks and nuns pray eight times daily, and you better not be late.) And all three religions honor "Father Abraham." Thus, politically, the marriage might have worked, but Jews, fearing being brought under Mohammed's theological umbrella, became belligerent—to the point where they began debunking this new religion. Who was this Johnny-come-lately who claimed to have the inside track? The Jews heard it as "my spin is better than your spin." Their attitude, at first one of diffidence, eventually turned to derision, and as you might expect, this did not sit well with our merchant-prophet—and now poet. The wrinkle in this tapestry is that Islam, though stating that all religions are one, has never forgiven its Jewish desert brothers.

With a Koran under his belt—not to mention a sword—and divine kinship established, the rejection by the Jews was the straw that broke the camel's back. (You have to allow the professor just one of these.) With that, Mohammed declared Islam independent and commanded his followers to pray toward Mecca and not Jerusalem.

Around the 9th century, as Greek books were translated into Arabic, Muslims began to be influenced by Greek science and philosophy. As they studied these along with mathematics and medicine, Muslim philosophers emerged and turned their new knowledge toward the study of God. However, rather than tempting them to abandon their Koran, they used this to demonstrate a connection between their holy writings and science. At the outset, these philosophers believed that the God of the Greeks was the same as their Allah; but over time, and with much study, they came to believe their new rationalism could generate an even higher form of God than the Allah of the Koran..

Today, philosophers and scientists are sometimes seen as questioners—even attackers—of God, but the Muslim philosophers had no wish to destroy Islam. Instead, they aimed to purge it of its primitive roots, thus making it more pure. God's existence was a given, but now they needed to prove it logically; for only by doing that could they make Allah and rationalism acceptable bedfellows. God was someone who could be revealed by peeling back layers of logic—not a God that was revealed only to a few specific people over time.

The first of this wave of Muslim thinkers was al-Kindi who lived during the middle of the 9th century. He sailed right through ye olde academic trap of "publish or perish" by a huge (and very influential) amount of writing and embraced Aristotle's notion of God as a perfect being who created everything that appears on earth. He was followed by a second philosopher, al-Razi, a physician, who rejected Aristotle's and al-Kindi's notion of God as prime mover. He also tossed out the Koran's emphasis on revelation and prophecy, taking the position that only philosophy and reason could explain God. (There's great comfort in rationalism though it rarely quickens the heart.)

Now comes the millennium, which by the way, many believers thought would signal the end of the world. A Turkish physician, al-Farabi—also musician, philosopher and mystic— was concerned about just how the uneducated masses with scant reasoning ability, could be saved. His solution? Revelation was a matter of the heart not head—an entirely natural event; this explains how Mohammed had revealed God to his people in such a simple manner. After all, al-Farabi was in sync with Plato's having defined the ideal ruler of a society as someone grounded in rational principles. And was not philosophy simply a better way to understand those basic truths that prophets had always expressed in poetry and metaphors? (Rationalist though he was, al-Farabi died early of alcoholism and excessive sex, irrefutable proof that burning the candle at both ends was not limited to Roman emperors or their modern day counterparts—punk rockers and movie stars.)

Jewish philosophers start to surface

While writing in Arabic, too. Go figure.

Yiddish folklore maintains "when two Jews get together, you have three opinions." (By contrast, my mother simplified my father's life by limiting his choices in suits to either blue or brown.) Ibn-Joseph was one of those trying to square the personal God of the Talmud with Islam's rational God. Ibn-Joseph was a fervent believer, but argued that the idea of creation from nothing had no rational basis; moreover, that we might not be able to understand God in rational terms alone. Besides, our limited human language could simply not capture the reality and grandeur of God. A century or so later, another Jewish philosopher, Ibn-Gabirol also tossed out the idea of creation evolving from nothing. God was clearly in charge, though the how and why remained a mystery.

Toward the end of the 11th century, still another Jewish philosopher, Pakudah, averred that the world had not happened by accident, but that God had, in fact, created it—in a moment in time. (Moment in that sense may be the same as TV's ubiquitous "our show will continue in just a moment.")

Careful readers will have noted that in these early days, physicians were often philosophers as well, this due, no doubt, to their having leisure time to indulge their thought processes rather than fretting over rising malpractice premiums.

There were still other Muslim philosophers and theologians. All of them struggled trying to explain God in ways that made sense (if only to themselves). One of these, Al Ghazzali, believed it was impossible to prove God's existence through logic and rationality. Still another philosopher-physician, Judah Halevi in 12th century Spain agreed in part: God could not be proved logically, but—this was not the same as saying that *belief* in God was irrational. It was just that a logical explanation had no real religious value. Anyway, he added, only the prophets knew anything about God.

We need to take note of one influential Muslim philosopher who weighed in toward the end of the 12th century—ibn-Rushd. He argued that rationalism and religion went hand in glove. However, he said the philosophical study of religion was only for the elite, and if the masses tried it, their salvation was doomed. (That would be enough to scare the faithful away from thinking forever—which is actually not that far off from what the early church attempted to do.) More important, ibn-Rushd influenced many who followed him, including two stalwarts who loom large in historical theology—St. Thomas Acquinas and Moses Maimonides.

Let's take the second of these first. Maimonides, a Spanish rabbi and philosopher, was forced to flee from Spain by the Berber persecution. However, he felt no animosity toward Islam, and in his landmark work, *The Guide for the Perplexed,* Maimonides states that the faith of the Jews was completely rational and not an arbitrary set of rules. An understanding of God would not yield to human reason. Seminal thinker though he was, Maimonides still preferred the God of the Bible to the God of the philosophers, saying that you could learn more about God from imagination than from your intellect.

(Today's seminaries of all faiths would do well to encourage students to give rein to the former and exercise reasonable restraint with the latter. Too often, the discipline of systematic theology can over reach and spin itself into an endless loop of debates leading nowhere, one professor describing it as something akin to "sawing sawdust.")

Back to Maimonides—Jewish communities of southern France and Spain were quick to adopt his ideas. Then, in the 13th and 14th centuries, western European Christians set about to drive Islam from Spain and succeeded. Tragically, in so doing they transplanted the noxious weed of Western European anti-Semitism to Spain and thereby destroyed the Jewish community.

Marranos was the name given to those Jews who were forced to convert or die, but continued to observe the high holy days secretly in underground chambers. Some historians believe Christopher Columbus was a Marrano. If so, before he sailed, I'm sure his mother made him take his raincoat, or whatever they called it then.

The advent of the ontological proof

Theology has always loved big words

The 11th century saw religious philosophy start to lose ground among Muslims and Greeks. It also marked the Battle of Hastings the date of which has been seared into my mind ever since the eighth grade. I might forget my PIN number but never 1066. In sum, the ontological proof defines God as "that about which no greater can be thought." In talk show parlance: God is the greatest. With God now defined as an object of thought, it was our privilege and right to think about and understand God.

Arguably, the best known and most respected religious philosopher of this period was corpulent in body and stoic in mind—plus being a man of few words, the latter quality earning St. Thomas Acquinas the nickname of "the dumb ox." Hardly. In his masterful work, *Summa Theological I and II.* Acquinas tried to meld this new philosophy into traditional Western Christianity. His approach was to define God in the same way that God had defined himself to Moses when he said "I am what I am." (I used to puzzle over this but then I recalled my Mother's response to my childhood question, "what are we having for dinner?" *We're having what we're having. Now go wash up.*

Acquinas went on to say that God is not just another being like us, but in fact—*being* itself. The impact of his thought upon the Catholic world was enormous, centering on his five "proofs" that God existed. (1) a proof that there must have been a beginning. (2) Ibn-Sina's argument that there had to be a necessary being (3) Aristotle's original proof of a prime mover (4) an argument that what we see in the world *cannot* be due to chance and (5) Aristotle's observation that the beauty and excellence of the creation had to come from a perfection for which there is no equal. Acquinas' work has been described as the "rational naturalism of man as seen through a stained glass window."

The proofs of Acquinas' great mind are largely ignored today, perhaps because they define God as just another (higher) step or layer in existence. This tempts us to see God as being created in our image—a kind of heavenly Superman which tends to raise more questions than it answers. Understandably, as the 14th century got underway, there was a lot of grumbling among theologians who, though they personally accepted God's existence, realized they had fallen short in their goal of using the key of rationalism to unlock theology's fortress-like door.

CHAPTER 3

A BRIEF HISTORY OF GOD (PART II)

The roots of mysticism

Bearing flowers, fruit and a lot else

Mystics have always been with us. They undergo wardrobe changes, makeup, dialect, even physical movement and posture, but myth matters. Its role is to provide nourishment and a welcome time-out from rationalism, which can grow a little stale like day-old biscuits. Even though the early prophets decried mythology—God was right here and now—monotheism still offered mystical overtones. Thus, God was positioned as being more than human: in other words, neither *like* us nor *of* us. Though the thinkers of the age of Acquinas would be surprised, societies today seem to tolerate and find a warm spot in their hearts and wallets for mystics and mystical religion. Consider the millions of devotees of Zen, the large devoted followings of charismatic mystics such as the Bagwan Rashneesh, the rapid growth of the charismatic church in America, the Hari Krishna cult and finally, the renewed interest in Buddhism. The latter is happily immune to those "unprovable" issues about God's existence that have kept philosophers awake at night.

Jewish mystics were on the scene as early as the 2nd and 3rd centuries, a good hundred years before Christianity emerged as a separate and full-blown monotheism. Mystical religion appealed to those who had no interest in pondering God's existence or identity. "Works for me" was their credo. Scholars call this early movement *Throne Mysticism*. Clearly, it worked for many, lasting more than a thousand years, finally being subsumed into Kabbalah, the Jewish mysticism of the 13th century. To get to the throne of God, Throne Mystics had to travel through the "seven heavens." These concepts echo Ezekiel and his chariot—metaphorical symbols that allowed one to "soar" spiritually. Seven centuries later, Talmudic scholars would not permit young people to study Kabbalah unless they were both intelligent and mature. Also, a mystic had to be married—to prove his sexual maturity as well. For some, Kabbalah held the promise (or threat) of "tripping out." The journey might be fun and all that, but getting back was another story.

The most unlikely mystic, if you can believe this, was a Pope, one Gregory by name. Not even wanting the job, he took it and made one of his non-religious priorities rebuilding Rome, trying to restore the quality of life to a city that had become a disaster area. But his reputation was that of a spiritual "master." He "hid" God in a safe darkness comprised of the metaphors of fog, darkness and clouds; and he did this to prevent humans from gaining any real knowledge of God. Just across the Adriatic, the Greeks were back in business, peddling their own brand of mysticism into the heart of a buyer's market. No more visions or images—just concentration and contemplation. In fact, in the 5th century, a bishop named Diodochus, taught his followers to concentrate by breathing. The logic was that the more slowly you breathed, the more you could focus your attention inwardly. Of course, Oriental philosophers had known about this kind of thing for centuries. (One is reminded of how medical practitioners in America came belatedly, not to mention, begrudgingly, to acknowledge the legitimacy of acupuncture.)

But there's more to philosophy than Greece and Rome. Ideas cross over borders like the wind, and thus in the 12th century, we find a Persian mystic, Suhrawardi, who had devoted his life to linking Oriental religion with Islam. (Ibn-Sina, whom we met earlier, had already proposed this sort of hook-up.) Suhrawardi experienced God as light, the only divine metaphor that made sense for him. He believed that visions and symbols (such as heaven and hell) were as real as anything we saw on earth, but they could only be experienced by someone with the necessary training. People pondered this in their heart of hearts: *you're telling me that since I'm not trained, the best I can do is to imagine God.* Suhrawardi nodded yes, saying that imagination was the only meaningful way to explain the reality of God, and all the religious symbols which stand for things we cannot see. And the people said hmm.... No matter where you stand on this, it seems that God (your definition) is an absent reality, yet one that has influenced people since the dawn of time.

Enter Sophia

A woman takes center stage

And wonder of wonders, it took an Arab male, Ibn-al-Arabi, to pull it off! Our hero lived on the Euphrates River, and upon reaching 40, he saw a young woman, Nizam, in a vision. He picked her out of a lineup of gods and goddesses with no hesitation: this was Sophia, the divine wisdom.

(You have to hear this. About ten years ago, a large group of church women of several mainline denominations held a national conference in Wisconsin and all affirmed the importance of Sophia. They also stood outside and prayed to the moon, making strange sounds, thus incurring the ire of those congregations back home who were footing the bill. This sent shock waves

through, among other churches, the United Methodists. John Wesley would have been sorely troubled, but then, the little guy from Epworth happened to believe in ghosts.)

For the record, ibn-al-Arabi was quite serious about his vision and he was persuaded that we could never find and love God by relying on rational philosophic logic alone but would wind up in a blind alley. The only way we could really see God was by his being revealed through someone like Nizam. Moreover, he held that mystics had an obligation to themselves to create epiphanies (such as his own) so they might come to know God's love and creativity. What is perhaps most noteworthy about ibn-al-Arabi is his extreme tolerance of other religions. He held that Allah's face could be seen everywhere. Sadly enough, this blend of mysticism and inclusiveness was too complex for most people to comprehend.

Now a quick segue to Turkey where tourists watch (and click) in amazement as the whirling dervishes take to the air. What's even more amazing is that this dance was devised as a means of spiritual concentration. Originally, the dancers belonged to the order of Mawlawiyyah (that's a name you don't mess around with) founded about the middle of the 13th century by Jalal al-Din-Rumi, who hailed from central Asia. His brand of mysticism was perceived as a Muslim response to the invasion by Turkey of the Mongols, i.e., a way to persuade Muslims that Allah had not forsaken them. Like others we've mentioned, Rumi believed God could only be experienced subjectively and accordingly, devoted his life to finding the reality of God's love and beauty in everything. What more apt and fervent metaphor than a whirling dance! Think of it as a ballet for the soul.

Meanwhile in Eastern Europe, the violent anti-Semitism had boiled over into persecution, reaching a level that brought the Ashkenazi (European) Jews to the brink of despair. Perhaps mysticism would offer some relief, and Rabbi Judah (known as the Pietist) came to the fore. Rather than dwelling on theological niceties, the Pietist mystics focused on down-to-earth issues. Concentration and silence, they believed, were essential to experience God, an idea we've seen several times before; and their mysticism took them beyond the semantic dimensions of liturgy to assigning a numerical value to each Hebrew letter.

Kabbalah, this symbolic interpretation of God, was passed on from teacher to student and so on. Its followers (Kabbalists) looked upon the glory of God from the outside and tried to reach the *inner* life of God. Eschewing rationalism, like Maimonides, for them, imagination was the conduit to God. Kabbalists distinguished between the God of creation and revelation and the hidden God who is unknowable. The resulting complex mythology is built around a tree containing ten enumerations of the divine reality. Every word of the Bible referred to one of these ten enumerations, and each biblical verse had a mirror verse in the life of God.

The inevitable book was forthcoming—The *Zohar,* written toward the end of the 13th century by a mystic from Leon. The author, rabbi Shinor ben Yochai, had studied Maimonides and then discovered Kabballah. *The Zohar* tells the story of a third century Talmudist trekking around the Middle East, talking to his disciples about God. Hardly systematic in his development, it explains the ten enumerations as a process each mystic must undergo. First, you must understand yourself completely which will enable you to become aware of God's presence. Only then can a mystic go beyond the artificial limits and restraints of personality and ego. This kind of thinking wouldn't hold up under a close, literal examination, but what counted is that Kabbalah, with its energy and fervor, provided a lot of psychological support to the 15th century Jews of Spain. Things could not have been worse for them, and they embraced this as a gift from God.

Christian mysticism developed a little more slowly, and several names come to mind: Gertrude, Suso and Eckart in Germany, and in England, Julian and Hampole. Again, there are books galore about each and all of these. But our favorite is Meister Eckart, and we'll get into him by way of something that as you have been told, is near and dear to my heart, i.e., flying.

Perhaps you have heard the old saw, "There are old pilots and bold pilots, but no old, bold pilots." The same might hold true for outspoken mystics, and the one we have in mind is Meister Eckart. One Sunday morning in the city of Cologne, Meister was walking down the street, carrying a lit candle and a bucket of water. One prominent burger asked him the purpose of this, and Meister replied, "With the candle I am going to burn up heaven, and with the water, I am going to douse the fires of hell...and then we'll see."

"See what, Herr Eckart?"

"Then we'll see who *really* loves God."

The Dominican friar was straightaway arrested for heresy, among other things, for denying that God was good. Eckart rejected the literal notion of the Trinity out of hand saying it was a mythical idea, in which God created only Jesus' *soul.* Further, he asserted that one's intellect could cause him to see God as three different persons, but that once mystics were joined with God, they would see him as one.

Wrap-up

As we've learned, for the last three or four centuries, Muslim teachers and scholars had all come to the belief that rational logic was useless in studying God; and by now, in much of Islam, the mystics were in the saddle and riding hard. Because of its rich and moving symbolism, it went down easier (like medicine with a spoonful of sugar) than did the old traditional approaches to God.

In 1256, an English Franciscan monk and philosopher and shade-tree chemist named Roger Bacon, made a mixture of 40% saltpeter, and 30% each of carbon and sulphur, and called it gunpowder. The only problem is: he couldn't figure out what to do with it. Just like a philosopher.

Meanwhile, Western Europe's brand of mysticism continued to lag behind, and now, the Kabbalists in the West were gaining in strength. There was a new wave of rationalism forming out in the swells. The Protestant reformers of the new century were gathering strength, the huge breakers soon to come crashing ashore, pounding all who stood in their path.

Discoveries, inventions and other debacles

Renaissance and revolution

"May you live in interesting times." The ancient Chinese were never quite sure whether this was a blessing or a curse. In the 15th and 16th centuries, Europe came in for its fair share of both. The Italian Renaissance burst into full flower; Columbus stepped ashore on what is now the Dominican Republic, convinced he had found the route to India. (Spices were the hot new currency.) And the scientific revolution was well underway. In France, a 17-year-old farmer's daughter heard God's voice tell her to save the king, and Joan of Arc led an army to defeat England at Orleans. For her heroism, she would wind up burned at the stake and later deified *by the same church.*

Meanwhile, Catholics and Protestants would begin a battle for the hearts and minds of millions of people—one that is still going on to this day. The Turks, fiercest of all warriors, conquered Constantinople, the Byzantine Empire giving its last gasp. The Muslims were driven from Spain, and now with Catholics in charge, hundreds of thousands of Jews fled the country in panic. To stay meant suffering the horrors of the Inquisition: forcible baptism or death. Change was in the air and conflict the order of the day; and the way that the three major religions defined and worshipped their God would be profoundly affected by these and other events.

With the emergence of The Ottoman Empire in Turkey, the Moghuls in India and the Safavids in Persia, this time around, the Muslims were in the driver's seat and strengthened their position even more. The Ottomans regarded their Christian sub-

jects less favorably than they had historically and made no secret of it. In Persia, Mir Damad launched a more contemporary
faith that followed the core beliefs of our old friend, the 12th
century mystic, Suhrawardi, emphasizing the psychological aspects of religion. Mulla Sadra, a pupil of Mir Damad, believed
that God was the source of everything—the prime mover—and
taught that knowing God was something to be done in this world,
not the next one. Mulla Sadra's parting gift to historical theology was the fascinating notion that there was an individual God
for each person that was to be found in that person's imagination. And there was also an individual heaven for each person
as well. (Six billion plus heavens would take up a lot of room;
thus I'm relieved this didn't catch on.) Plus, no two Gods and
no two heavens were alike. Acquinas and Augustine would surely
have turned over in their graves!

Despite these radical—some say revolutionary—currents
of thought, Islam still maintained its tolerance and respect for
other faiths. Would that the same could be said for European
Christianity. In the 15th century, the Ashkenazi (European) Jews
were thrown out of Vienna, Cologne, Bavaria, Linz, Augsburg,
Milan, Tuscany and Moravia, just as the Sephardic Jews were
expelled from Spain. In Portugal, worse still: Jews found outside the "ghetto" after dark would be whipped through the
streets.

The new Kabbalism

A healing fervor takes hold

The psychic and physical wounds of these persecutions went
deep; and recognizing the need for healing, two Jewish spiritual leaders, Karo and Alkabaz, migrated to Safed in Galilee
and developed a new form of mystical Kabbalism. The old
Kabbalism was for the elite, but this new form was for all Jews,
and its intensity, both healing and heartening, touched the community in a way that Talmudic (Jewish law) study never had. In
a phenomenal burst of imagination, the new Kabbalah made

homelessness equal to Godliness. Thus the Jews, many of whom had become wanderers searching for safe haven, knew God still had his eye upon them.

It is no wonder, then, that this new Kabbalah grew like wildfire, not only in Galilee among the Sephardic exiles but also in Europe among the Ashkenazi. Fearing that its teachings—popular, daring, perhaps even dangerous—would be taken literally, its teachers wrote with restraint and caution. One of these, Isaac Luria, a late 15th century Kabbalist leader, took on a paradox that monotheists had wrestled with for centuries and come up empty-handed: how could a perfect God have created a world full of evil?

Luria' s answer was an ingenious alloy of imagination and logic: God had created a place within himself and left it vacant—in short, a place where God was *not!* Further, God could and would fill this empty space with revelation (evidence of himself) and creation (physical life). But God would remain absent from this place—an exile from the vacant part of himself and *therefore not associated with the evil that existed.* Seldom has one thought had such impact upon a people or philosophy, for this brand of Kabbalah was able to diffuse the anger of the Jews against the world's harsh treatment for them. Moreover, it created within them a far more positive and accepting view of society.

The darkness descends

Plagues and persecutions

Contemporary Christians had not escaped hardship and disaster themselves. (In mid 14th century Europe and Asia, over a period of 20 years, 1 of every 3 persons died from the plague— some estimates go higher.) There was also the Avignon Captivity and the loss of Constantinople, but the religious writings of the time were absent the balm of healing. Instead, writers such as Gerson and Scorns focused on God's power and dominion and maintained that humans were helpless to assure their salvation. Moral behavior was not good in and of itself, but only because God had said it was. This trend picked up momentum from the Renaissance philosophers and humanists who criticized medieval religion which in their view was "left-overs" that served God up as being too boring and removed from everyday life. Though the energy of the Renaissance lent an initial impetus to learning, the notion that God was far beyond human reach took hold in the minds of many. Some said it was as though the world had been a clock that God had wound up, then went off and left. But the worst was yet to come....

At about the time of Columbus' voyage, the new pope to be, Innocent VIII, made a solemn vow not to name more than one member of his family to high office. However, as soon as he took office, he declared, with equal solemnity, that since papal power was supreme, he was not bound by his oath. History records that he was the first pope to acknowledge several of his illegitimate children, on whom he heaped honors and great wealth. The sale of indulgences was thriving (buying your way out of Purgatory) and as if this were not bad enough, he published a Papal Bull, *Summa Desiderantes.* This amounted to a witch hunt, and the persecutions that followed led to the death of hundreds of innocent women. Among these was the infamous Black Mass, which worshipped the Devil. Historians blame ignorance and anti-Semitism coupled with a bizarre misreading of the Koran. A few kinder scholars have tried to excuse Innocent's behavior, but most agree these events marked the worst perversion of Christianity since the Crusades.

The German Reformation

A priest takes on the Pope

His name was Martin Luther. (It had been Ludher, but he later changed it, wanting something more dignified.) A German monk whose father had wanted him to be a lawyer, Luther suffered from a tortured soul. (Although called the "Father of the Reformation," it was Erasmus of Rotterdam who actually led the first charge into battle with the Vatican.) On the plus side of the ledger, the upstart priest took on Rome with a fearlessness that made others question his sanity. To disgrace the upstart priest, Pope Leo X floated the rumor that Luther was the result of the devil's union with Luther's mother in the bathhouse at Eiseleben. Not to be undone, Luther underwent a trial, then escaped prosecution and while in hiding, translated the New Testament from the Latin into German thus making the Bible accessible to his countrymen. Central to this new theology was his doctrine of "justification by faith," which meant in part, only God, not man, could save humanity, a doctrine some maintain was recycled from Catholicism a century earlier.

Popularized versions of Luther's announcing his split with Rome have him "nailing" his 95 theses to the church door at Wittenburg. In truth, he simply posted an announcement of the debate—normal procedure for academics of that time. (Today, we'd use a push-pin.)

Had it not been for the inventive genius of a man born Johannes Gensfleisch, some scholars question whether Luther would have gotten off the ground. Gensfleisch came up with the idea of movable type and ran off some copies of Luther's diatribe, one of which fell into the hands of Pope Leo X. Our printer, sensing this was hot copy and that fame was in the offing, and not wanting to be remembered as John Gooseflesh, adopted the name of his hometown, Gutenberg. And, as they like to say, all the rest is history.

Like it or not, we have to deal with the contradictions of arguably the most controversial—not to mention conflicted—figure in the history of God. Whereas the Kabbalist, Luria, taught that God was to be found in joy and peace, Luther declared that knowing God lay in suffering and the cross, a darkness against which the cleverness of theologians would avail them naught. Though early on, he had invited rabbis to colloquies for their help in translating the Old Testament, he later became a virulent anti-Semite. Though repulsed by sex and a hater of women, at 42, Luther married an ex-nun Katerina Von Bora, moved into an abandoned monastery, fathered six children and presided over a household with boisterous parties. His venomous tract, *Of the Jews and Their Lies,* remains one of the most savage attacks on Jews ever written and morphed into his last sermon, delivered three days before his death at age 53. Apologists for Luther have said, "God sent us an angry man for an angry age," but that only begs the question. How could such wrath and hatred flourish within a man who said he loved God? To this day, the question has never been satisfactorily answered.

The Swiss Reformation

The search for purity and piety

It's a short hop from Germany to Switzerland, but what a leap of the mind, from Luther to John Calvin. This man of small build and sallow features is credited as the author of the second Reformation which led to, you guessed it, Calvinism. (Most belief systems apparently end in "ism").

Let's get to the man and his ethos: simply put, humans could achieve whatever they wanted to achieve. These beliefs ushered in the English Puritans in the 17th century, which segued into the colonization of the New World. Calvin's Christianity believed that God existed as three "persons," and to make sure everyone got the message, put to death a Spanish theologian, Servetus, who denied the Trinity. (Calvin had also declared there was nothing in the New Testament which contradicted the Jewish monotheistic writings.) In his latter years, Calvin suffered from gout, hemorrhoids, chronic asthma, headaches and indigestion. Never sleeping more than four hours a night, he churned out a volume of work that boggled the mind—then and now. He adored books, and therefore knowledge, and beauty, and rather than the haughty, arrogant, joyless stereotype history has made him out to be, Calvin was the most profound and sensitive thinker the Reformation produced.

In his will he defined himself as a "pitiable creature" and a "miserable sinner" but one who loved God. We can only take John Calvin at his word, for today, four hundred years later, Calvinism still lives, proof that *isms,* of whatever ilk, die hard.

Yet another Swiss theologian, the Italian Socinus, injected some radical ideas about the Reformation. First, the concept of Jesus as the Son of God did not mean a divinity but only that God had a special love for Jesus. Second, that instead of dying for man's sins, Jesus was a teacher of salvation; and third, the idea of a Trinity was an imagined concept that, regrettably, prompted people to think of three separate Gods. Socinus' ideas went over the edge for the Swiss—who have always been cautious to a fault—and under pressure from the Calvinists, he moved to Transylvania where his teachings formed the theological cornerstone for the Unitarians!

Calvin died in 1564 (the year of Shakespeare's birth) and his followers thought they needed to separate Calvinism from both the Lutherans and Catholics. That task fell to Calvin's former principal assistant, Beza, who declared that God had decided to save some people but "predestine" the rest to eternal damnation. Thus man's salvation was *entirely* in God's hands. Ironically, though Calvin is synonymous with predestination, the concept has alarmed countless others who reason thusly: if we believe everything in the Bible, then the God of the Bible is responsible for every single action on earth. And that brings us right back to God sanctioning—worse yet, *creating*—evil. Anyway, you look at it, it's an unhappy paradox for the Calvinists.

Wrap-up

The engine of reform that revved up for two centuries finally wound up in a ditch of fear and enmity, with the Catholics on one side and Protestants on the other. They may have thought alike at times, but their behavior indicated otherwise. Unlike the new Kabbalah of Isaac Luria, Catholic and Protestant theologies had not allayed the people's fears about life but rather poured fuel on the fire.

Calvin had angered not a few when he stepped over the line of Christian doctrine and said the biblical creation story was for the simple and uneducated and should not be taken literally. On the other hand, the Catholic Church had threatened Galileo with death when he declared that Copernicus was right: the earth revolved about the sun, not the other way around. The Pope made him recant and put him under house arrest, and it was not until centuries later that the church admitted its error.

At the same time that Mulla Sadra told Muslims that heaven and hell were in the imaginary world, Catholic leaders were arguing that both of these had definite locations. And while the Kabbalists were told not to take the myth of creation literally, Catholics and Protestants were preaching that the biblical accounts were literally true. If people back then kept score—and I rather imagine some did—it was likely that the people who believed God was a fact of life (like everything else on earth) were winning against those who believed God could only be found through imagination and contemplation.

Once again, religious schools of thought grated against each other like tectonic plates in the earth. Fault lines began to appear as dogma was brought into question and doctrines given close scrutiny under the light of reason. Enlightenment was blowing in the wind.

God in the 17th and 18th centuries

Science sets out to prove his existence

Why should the proof of God be any different than a mathematical proof? This sums up the reasoning of the great minds of science, among these, Rene Descartes, a French Catholic mathematician. He thought that upon examination he would find the universe carefully assembled each piece in place, but no such luck. Nature was random, disorganized and at times it seemed that God should hang a sign on the door, "Temporarily Out of Order" Descartes took a step back and trotted out the ontological proof of Anselm (check your mental notes) and reasoned thusly: since we know it takes a concept of perfection to point out imperfections, this concept of perfection could be none other than the perfect God. Therefore, God does exist. End of proof.

Another such luminary was Blaise Pascal of a similar bent and background who had been a child prodigy. But unlike Descartes, he had a deeply moving mystical experience as an adult and was convinced the true God was one of revelation, not one of the philosophers as he first thought. Therefore, there was really no way to *prove* that God existed. Indeed, Pascal's skepticism was such that some scholars claim he was the first person to question seriously whether there was a God at all. One day a friend who was fond of gambling posed the question: "what are the odds of rolling 2 sixes at least once in 24 rolls of the dice?" Pascal solved the problem and is remembered more as the father of probability theory than as a theologian.

Across the channel in England, Isaac Newton attempted to explain God using his famed theory of gravity. He asked himself why the same gravitational force which pulled the stars and planets together did not keep on pulling them together until they became one mass. Ah, hah, reasoned Newton. The cause must lie in a divine power (his words: intelligent agent) that kept the heavens from imploding. Newton did not like mysteries, and there is no known mention of the Bible in Newton's writing. To the contrary, he worked hard to extract the mysteries from Christianity and in the process found himself in conflict with the divinity of Jesus and the Trinity. In Newton's view, the Trinity was a false concept the church had used to impress and thus convert pagans. Moreover, Jesus had not been a God but a prophet sent to teach the truth. As a result of his position, Newton served as a likely catalyst for modern religion's skepticism.

Problem: if you removed the mythology and the mystery that enhanced the image of God, what was left would have scant appeal to Christians...you can see where this is going. At about the time of the American Revolution (and The Enlightenment) Voltaire's response was to define his concept of the ideal religion in his *Philosophical Dictionary.* Like his contemporaries, he rejected the cruel Christian God who promised eternal fire. Also tossed out were those Biblical mysteries that defied logic. At the same time, however, they retained their faith in a Supreme Being and gave the cold shoulder to atheism which they thought was sheer superstition.

European Jews were exuberant over these new ideas. One of these was Spinoza, a Dutch Jew of Sephardic extraction. Disenchanted with the study of Torah, in the middle of the 17th century he presented ideas that differed radically from the Judaism of the time. Even though he credited Descartes with having shaped his thoughts, the Amsterdam synagogue was not impressed and threw him out. Now a religious free agent, Spinoza became the model for a wave of secular thought that would become the underpinning of Western religious philosophy. Simply put—if you'll let me get by with that—Spinoza saw God as merely the sum of all the eternal laws of the universe; in other words, when we spoke about God, we were talking about the mathematical laws that governed our very existence. Clerics shrugged and the Pope frowned, but men like Descartes and Spinoza paid them little heed. God had given them a brain and not to use it was an insult to the Creator.

As the 18th century reached its mid point, a former Jewish silk merchant from Berlin turned philosopher formulated a view of God that side stepped the prevalent Christian obsession with biblical doctrine. Moses Mendelsohn's God was personal, like their God of the Bible, exemplifying the qualities of love, justice, wisdom and goodness. He reasoned further that if revelation were the sole key to knowing God, then many might be denied this joy. Therefore, making God more like us would allow anyone with common sense to know him. Mendelsohn's grandson, Felix, would thrill listeners with his sublime music in the years to come. Having said that, the grandfather's theology resonated with an audience hungry for a new vision of an old God.

Two years before the signing of the Declaration of Independence, the Russian-born philosopher, Immanuel Kant published his *Critique of Pure Reason* and struck a blow for freedom from the doctrinal shackles that had ruled for so long: the path to God, said Kant, lay in moral conscience. The ceremonial trappings, rituals, church authority and formal prayers only kept people from relying on themselves and their own engines of moral imperative. Arguments for God's existence are interesting but not useful. And why? Because man's reason fades beyond the dimensions of our own space and time. One of the great philosophers of the age, Kant passionately believed in God, but he stated that man could neither prove nor disprove the *existence* of God. Echoing Mendelsohn in part, Kant's model relegated God to a role in an ethical system that rewarded good deeds with happiness. (Interestingly enough, Kant's first name means "God with us.")

If when seeing a Hassidic (also spelled Chasidic) Jew with his black clothing, long beard, side curls and black hat, you think that a somber spirit dwells underneath you couldn't be more wrong. Their religion was positive and exuberant even in the face of adversity—the Polish pogroms, for example, that were essentially organized slaughters. Pogrom comes from a Russian word meaning "like thunder," and the hooves of the Cossacks' horses must have sounded like that as the marauders swept into the tiny villages or *shtetls* (rhymes with kettles).

In the 1640's, Israel ben Eliezer, a poor teacher of children, led the exodus of spiritual Jews out of Poland to escape these horrors. It was, in fact, the charismatic nature of their beliefs and worship that helped fuel their flight to safety. To them, God's presence filled the world like wine did a Sabbath dinner goblet; thus it was possible for devout Jews to experience God in practically everything they did (including lovemaking).

Spinoza had said that everything was God. The Hassids took this one step further: *God gave everything life!* The fervor of the message caused this new Hassidism to spread quickly, Eliezer urging his flock to laugh, dance and sing, while reminding them that "God requires no synagogues except in the heart." In a more formal vein, the theology of Hassidism stated that God was not a reality external to life but that God and man were interdependent.

Shifting currents in attitudes

Questions seeking answers

It should come as no surprise that Jews and Christians were not alone in weaning themselves off mysticism. In the late 18th century, an Arabian, al-Wahhab, set out to purge mysticism from Islam—and in his view, to purify it. He converted Muhammad ibn Saud, an ancestor of the current Saudi royal family. The movement focused on helping the poor and driving out idolatry. His doctrine insisted that no human should ever compete with God, thus in effect rejecting any notions of the divinity of Jesus. Within a hundred years, Wahabbism dominated Islam. More important, many scholars view it as the theological root of the radical Islamic movement in Saudi Arabia today. Apart and beyond from probing, proving or disproving God's existence, some had actually begun to *reject* God.

In the early 1700's, a priest, Jean Meslier, died after having "outed" himself as an atheist, and the Christian world gasped. Not only disheartened by his inability to believe in God, he was thoroughly disgusted with humanity in general. He thought that religion was used by the rich to oppress the poor, and that the doctrines of Trinity and the resurrection were both "ludicrous." Moreover, he was not alone. In Scotland at about the same time, David Hume said there was no reason to look beyond science to explain reality and no need to believe anything we couldn't experience. Hume believed that the world's evil was proof enough that God did not exist. And in France, a well-known philosopher, Diderot, had been imprisoned for espousing the same views. Diderot was indifferent about whether God existed or didn't. He saw no role for God as creator since nature had taken care of that. Finally, on the continent, Heinrich of Holbach published a book which later became known as "the bible of atheistic materialism."

What are we to make of this? In two centuries, the Western world experiences a religious "mood swing" from the ecstatic fervor of Hassidic Jewry, through a questioning of the validity of God, finally to wholesale rejection. Clearly, the attempts by both mystics as well as scientists to save God had largely failed. We're not implying that as the 19th century drew to a close, there were no believers left in the West—rather that atheism that began as a trickle was turning into a well-defined stream. Questioning God, once considered blasphemy (not to mention, dangerous to one's health) was now acceptable discourse in learned circles and elsewhere. At the very least, for believers, this was unsettling; what if the stream turned into a flood?

Atheism gains an audience

God in the obituary column

Hegel, Marx, Nietzsche and Freud. Change the names, and you could have the intellectual equivalent of the famous football players, the Four Horsemen of Notre Dame. Helmets or not, these four were heavyweights whose ideas would hit western civilization like a 300 pound linebacker. Had we put them into a small room, the discussion would have been lively at first, then growing steadily higher in volume. Yet, the one thing they shared in common was that they all found little use for God in their view of mankind. It was no secret that more people had been killed by "religious wars" than any other type of conflict. Horrific acts had been perpetrated in the name of the Western Christian God, not to mention wholesale repression of joy, sexuality and personal freedom. In light of that, atheism was looking better by the minute, at least certainly to these four and their growing number of disciples.

They had been preceded by the English poet, William Blake, who along with ushering in the Romantic movement in poetry, announced there was no natural religion—that God was an organism much like man. He didn't actually say "God was dead," but he came close. A German philosopher, Hegel, whose ideas were related to Kabbalah taught that Judaism was a base religion with a simplistic notion of God. Further, this God was a God who demanded obedience to useless laws. There's more: Judaism had done great damage and was the example of everything bad in religion. (At least we know where he stood.) Hegel stated that Jesus had tried to move beyond this "base religion" but that over time, Christians had regressed into once again believing in the divine God of the Old Testament.

Hegel' s rejection of God was mild compared to a German contemporary, Schopenhauer, a lecturer living in Berlin. He had no friends, never married and defined pleasure as merely the absence of pain. It's no wonder that for him, there was no God and no logic—moreover, the only important thing was the will to live. Like Hegel, he saw Judaism as simplistic, but he also tagged Islam as being yet another useless religion. The best we can say about Schopenhauer is that he refined pessimism into an art.

Karl Marx was the second member of this formidable "backfield." His ideology was blunt and to the point: God was irrelevant and could not help the world. Religion merely existed to make suffering bearable. His most oft-quoted line is that "religion is the opium of the people." Marx saw society as being in perpetual conflict—workers vs. owners, proletariat against capital. Thus, the Soviet Union did away with most of the church and then turned into a tyrannical religion without equal.

Our third member surfaces in the late 19th century bursting upon the scene with a pronouncement that rocked believers back on their heels. Wilhelm Friedrich Nietzsche, the son of a clergyman, mind you, announced that God was dead. The Christian God was a crime against life, said Nietzsche, because he encouraged people to fear their sexuality. He thought that a new race of men, a "superman" would save the world. The Nazis stole from his thinking, taking only what suited their inflated view of self destiny. By then, Nietzsche had gone quite mad.

Finally, comes the shy Viennese "alienist" who made psychoanalysis into a household word. In Freud's view, God was merely a construct of man's unconscious, and intelligent people would be advised not to pay attention. On the other hand, there was no need to abolish religion since intelligent people would outgrow it when they moved on to atheism; and the last piece of the puzzle would fall into place when science replaced God.

So much for the "backfield." Now let's move south to the Muslim world. Turmoil was the order—or disorder—of the day. The British and French had moved into North Africa with a vengeance, and before long, the Middle East would know the might of their heel. Since the Crusades, the European dislike and distrust of both Muslims and Jews qualified them as an equal-opportunity hater. Leading Muslim reformers felt Islam had to play catch up; thus they wanted to bring it kicking and screaming (though still kneeling) into the 20th century. There is a proverb that says "be careful what you wish for." Case in point—early 20th century Turkey. Mustafa Kemal (whom we know as Ataturk) subordinated Islam into a private religion sweeping it under a magic carpet of modernity. Religious schools were closed, traditional Islamic dress prohibited, and religious law and decree abolished. Later, in the 1930's, the Shah of Iran pulled off a similar move but with even more draconian measures.

Some Muslim reformers thought that Islam could be modernized with far less shock to the body politic, especially those who still clung to Islamic mysticism. An Egyptian, Muhammad Abduh traveled to Europe, his mind stimulated by what he absorbed. Abduh saw the Islamic texts as relics of a bygone era and insisted that along with the Koran, Muslims should be taught science and philosophy. They should focus on what God had created, not what God *was.* Farther east in India, the Muslim reform was spearheaded by Muhammad (we should be getting used to this name by now) Iqbal who was later knighted for his accomplishments. The holder of a doctorate from the West, Iqbal was dismayed by the decline of Islam in India: the new thrust should be on individual creativity to set loose the energy that lay within. This should not be likened to Nietzsche's absolute rejection of God or desire for a race of supermen. Rather, it was an appeal for humans to become *like* God in their behavior. After all, the earliest scriptures describe God as "making man in his image." Were we now to return the favor?

Putting God to the test

Some memories never die

Shifting to pre-Nazi Germany, the writer, Herman Cohen, stated that God was not a force that imposed his will on us, but rather an idea—a good idea but only that—formed in the mind of humans. As the ovens of the Holocaust attempted to burn out Jewish memory, the surviving remnant asked one question of their rabbis and each other: where was God in all this—if, indeed, he was there *at all*. Today, more than a half century later, some Jews reject out of hand the relevance of a God that allowed this to happen. Some firmly believe that the personal God of their ancestors, the God of Abraham, Isaac and Jacob, perished with their loved ones in the ultimate horror of the camps.

After the rubble was cleared, the evidence gathered, the trials held and the guilty punished, it was the consensus of many teachers and philosophers that this had not been God's finest hour. Indeed, he had not performed well at all. Seemingly, the God of the Bible had abandoned his people; the God of the philosophers and the mystics had ignored his job description; and the God of the Reformation and the Enlightenment had stood mute as a helpless witness to the annihilation of millions. This was but one more layer added to the atheism that was gaining a foothold in the popular mind-set. The evidence had been heard, the case tried and the jury was in.

Where to from here?

Mixed reviews

If we were intelligence operatives working for the CIA, we would submit what is called in spook jargon, a SitRep. Situation Report. And being objective about our work, our bottom-line evaluation would be, in a word, gloomy. The pluses are obvious: technology keeps on flowering with breakthroughs that benefit the many, not the least of which is in food production. The standard of living continues to rise in the developing world.

The cold war is over (though that seems like ancient history) and universal education is getting a leg up around the globe. Think of the astounding progress in the healing sciences; think of the great strides in entertainment and the arts; great increases in personal freedom and last, but surely not least, the avoidance of nuclear warfare. Think—but do not dwell upon it—for there is a minus side to the ledger.

And here the news is not good. Actually, frightening is the more appropriate term. Near the end of the millennium, we saw the use of germ and gas warfare by Iraq; the growing specter of the AIDS virus (some say visited upon us as punishment by God). Pestilence, famine and drought in Africa; a rising sea level; environmental pollution; a water shortage that borders on critical; a lower standard of living in many Third World countries; the lack of a health care delivery system where the need is most urgent; the emergence of terrorist institutions worldwide; collapse of democratic institutions worldwide; (there is no shortage of tyrants, petty or otherwise); and continued wars around much of the world.

To underscore what we have mentioned, AIDS has moved from what was a localized forest fire to a worldwide conflagration. A disaster that could rival or surpass the Great Plague. The threat of nuclear attack by rogue states whose bluster is backed up by an arsenal of frightening firepower. Wholesale and heavy-handed suppression of human freedom in China: the toxic spread of terrorism whose tentacles encircle the earth (more's the pity, much of it done in God's name); the impotency of peace efforts in the Middle East; massive famines in some Sub-Sahara countries where a crust of bread and a few ounces of water are often all that stand between life and death; and ecological disasters that erupt with each day's new headlines. Is anyone paying attention? Or is this just more than we can absorb and we punch the remote and search for relief. Obviously, and even to the most optimistic, the ledger is woefully out of balance. Make no mistake—we are in the red. Given the approach of this book, that begs two questions:

How could it all have turned out this badly if God (or his guidance system team) were at the controls?

Then depending on how you answer the above, here's the second:

Has God been a party to this. At all?

Let's rewind the tape to an 18th century statistician, Reverend Thomas Bayes who believed that God is revealed in his wondrous works; if so, the revelations of the latter fall woefully short. Indeed, they present a grotesque vision that should knock us to our knees. But in prayer? Or stunned disbelief? And at this point, if you subscribe to atheism in one form or another, you might offer up an "I told you so" though in a hushed voice—in case God is listening. Of course, if he's not, then where is this going?

Yes, in survey after survey, the vast majority of people say they believe in God. But that's like asking people do you believe in oxygen? "Well, sure," would come the answer, "but it's nothing to write home about." That's the problem. Believing in God is not the same as believing or trusting *on* God. This is starting to sound like a sermon, and since my ticket to ride that train has not been punched, I need to get off.

Let's zoom in on Europe for a moment. The great cathedrals in the largest cities are all but empty on Sunday mornings. Granted, church attendance has never been an accurate predictor of moral behavior. (The Nazi Wehrmacht marched into battle with *Gott mit Uns,* stenciled on their helmets: "God with us." Prior to that, here at home, Father Coughlin drew standing room only crowds as he spewed his rabid anti-Semitism like a broken sewer pipe. The Church remained silent.)

Was William Blake on target? And Nietzsche? Did they know something we don't—or won't admit? Or should we merely attribute that to manic depression? Was Schopenhauer's philosophy of pessimism an attitude or an affliction? These men were not by themselves in their dark view of a darkening world.

Scores of others, honored for their intellectual, artistic and scientific achievements, have joined in the battle cry. If God is not dead, then he must be hurtin' mighty bad. Bottom line? Evil is out there wherever you look, and if this is what God has wrought, then it's true that he has no future.

But the world still lives. With the horrific images of the pogroms scrawled in blood on their memory slates, the Hassidim danced their dances and sang their songs and hugged their hugs. Goodness has not been destroyed. Love will not die (even if others say God has). Social progress is being made, albeit more slowly than we, or God, would like. So...

So maybe God is not dead after all. Come to think of it—and think about it we must—maybe God has morphed, adjusted, adapted...become more relevant for more people. And still lives. Maybe just maybe, that's what God's future really is—an ever-changing, adaptive fluid relevance, given life and hope by our own revelation. Now that notion might elicit collective cardiac arrest on the part of the anti-Darwinists, not to mention some religious groups. But these are possibilities, and we can't walk away from them.

Let's shift to the boardroom. Those who run big companies (the honest ones) will tell you a tried and trusted business maxim: *you either change or die.* Having said that, if we think about one of the messages in this chapter, everyone we've talked about has been in the business of...well, changing God. Is it possible this might be the way God has avoided death ever since man uttered his first prayer? If it's possible, then we must give it serious consideration.

Stay with me. In his *Critique of Pure Reason,* our 18th century mentor, Kant, suggested that the path to God was moral conscience: not rituals, not the trappings of power, pomp and worship, not church authority...but people relying on themselves and their own moral engines. Much later, Martin Buber, another death of God theologian and disciple of Kant, refused to let go of the word God. He said he didn't know what other word to use to express what would otherwise would be an un-wieldy concept. Think of it as trying to catch the wind in a net.

Buber believed that we had to establish a lifelong dialogue with God and work out what God really meant and do this all by ourselves. Of course, the history of God, as we have seen, is replete with these kinds of dialectics and debates—knock down drag out fiery arguments after which, once the smoke has cleared, something old is tossed out and something new brought in. That is, after all, the way progress and change come about. It's the prime mover behind the development of this thing we call civilization.

On the other side of the table, sitting sternly in straight-backed chairs with solemn faces are the religious constructs. And they've been sitting there for centuries. Human counterparts of Stonehenge. A kind of religious Mount Rushmore where the frowns are etched in granite and dyspepsia writ large.

All right, it's troubling and painful and shameful and late in the game, but let's talk about it: take a moment to observe the many Catholics who have become disaffected, (and in many cases, disassociated) to the point of rage with a Church that excludes women from meaningful positions; a Church that maintains a condition of priesthood that clashes violently with current social norms, with predictably disastrous results. A Church that—well, you get the message. The Vatican is getting it too, but slowly.

One last business parallel. (After all, that's one ticket of admission I *do* have.) Let me state it as a maxim and give it its own space:

Religious belief systems which maintain absolute rigidity in the face of consequential, societal, psychological and environmental change run the risk of becoming obsolete in much the way that people stopped using railroads to move about.

ALL ABOARRRD! (Hey, where did all the people go?)

If that doesn't get your attention, then nothing else I can say will. (Ironically, the sad state of passenger airlines today is sounding the same two-minute warning. Either they change or...you finish the sentence.

You have been marvelously patient and diligent thus far. Now, I invite you to stay the course as we continue on our journey: examining alternative ways of defining God in the hope that each of us can develop a more comfortable, more relevant, more meaningful—and unique—relationship with a God concept that comports well with who each of us is (or wants to be).

APPENDIX TO
CHAPTERS 2 AND 3

This appendix is a review of chapters 2 and 3. Its purpose is to keep you attuned as to when and where the various concepts of God appeared in history and what kinds of baggage they brought with them. And I've taken the liberty of inserting a few noteworthy milestones from time to time that'll help you zoom out to keep the big picture in focus.

Capsule review of the history of God: Chapters 2 and 3

For those of you who feel reasonably comfortable with what we covered in these chapters, you can safely skip to page 79. If not, spend the next 6 minutes with us for what I hope is a useful review. (Jokes told earlier are expressly prohibited.)

Prehistoric:

People experience nature's (God's) wrath via storms, floods, drought, eclipses and the like. Human sacrifice is common. Worship of the mother goddess comes into vogue.

20,000 BCE: People speculate on cave walls about who or what lies behind this. It's called everything but art.

5000 BCE: Persians put forth belief that everyone has a spiritual counterpart in the sacred world "somewhere up there." Three thousand years later, Babylonians see their Gods as the source of their power.

Genesis (time unknown): We learn of Yahweh, the God of Moses and Abraham, the producer of miracles. The Rig Veda (Indian and Iran) describes a set of gods whose myths take the first exit from reality road. The Axial Age arrives, the Vedic gods decline and are replaced by Hinduism and Buddhism with a new position paper: Brahman is neither a deity nor does he talk to us.

3200 BCE: The Sumerians invent something called writing, and the first bill arrives in the mail—in the form of a thrown rock.

7th century BCE: The God of Isaiah demands meaning, not temple sacrifices. The same God foretells the destruction of Jerusalem. Isaiah 45:21, this God not only makes his first appearance but also says he does not have to explain himself to the people. The Greek philosophers conceive of a God in two parts: the essence of God about which we know nothing and God's power, which is evident to us here on earth.

55 BCE: Julius Caesar invades Britain.

1st century BCE: The rabbis bring the Decalogue (Mosaic Law) up to date and write it down.

1st century CE: Jesus born (6-4? BCE) Wanders about the Galilean hill country espousing a doctrine of inclusiveness, calling God, Abba ("beloved parent" in Aramaic). All of this puts him on a collision path with the religious and Roman authorities. After Jesus' death, a Jewish tentmaker positions Jesus as having replaced the Torah, though he never wrote a single word. Paul makes up for it, his letters comprising half of what would eventually become known as the New Testament.

47 CE: The first recorded use of the word "Christianity."

68: Josephus writes his *Antiquities*

70: Razing of the Jewish temple

67-73: First Jewish Roman War. Fall of Masada

120: Second Jewish-Roman War

2nd & 3rd century: Sabellius suggests that the one God of the Jews actually wears three masks: father, son and holy spirit. The idea of the Trinity is born. For his efforts, Sabellius is excommunicated by Pope Calixtus.

4th century: Gregory of Nyssa conceives of God as revealing himself in all three forms only when he wants to. Augustine refines God for the Catholic church, claiming God is not a physical reality but a spiritual presence in all.

Reign of King Arthur and His Knights of the Round Table

7th century: God reveals himself to Mohammed over a 23 year period. Islam's God tags idolatry as the root sin. Mohammed sees divinity as one and rejects Jesus as God's son. Core belief: the God of Islam created the world so we could know him, and we see him only in his actions. Muslim philosophers try to prove God's existence logically. Jewish philosophers try to square the personal God of the Jews with Islam's rational God. Some say although God cannot be proved rationally, *belief* in God *is* rational.

1000 CE: Leif Erikson discovers North America

1066-1270: The Crusades

11th century: A Spanish rabbi, Maimonides, teaches that understanding God won't yield to human reason. Q.E.D. You can learn more about God from imagination than from intellect. St. Thomas Acquinas defines God just as God had defined himself to Moses, "I am what I am." This is called the ontological proof of God. To Acquinas, God is not anthropomorphic (like us) but is being itself.

The Middle Ages: Mystics, who had been hanging out for a very long time, exert strong appeal to those who are too tired to ponder the question about God's existence: does he or doesn't he. They cloak God in darkness, vision and symbols. *You have to imagine God in this environment.* Jewish mystics adopt the Kabbalah as a symbolic interpretation of God with imagination providing the uplink.

1380: John Wycliffe translates the Bible into English.

1431: The church burns Joan of Arc at the stake.

1455: First printed Bible appears.

15th century: Pope Innocent VIII legalizes his own form of mysticism (witchcraft). Worst perversion of Christianity up until that time. A German monk, Martin Luther, adopts and massages it. The "Father of the Reformation" maintains God is in the dark and must be taken on faith. Calvin holds that God exists as three persons. Mulla Sadra, like Maimonides before him, says God is to be found in your imagination.

1584: A struggling English playwright produces *Hamlet*

1620: Pilgrims land at Plymouth Rock.

1692: Salem, Massachusetts—Pilgrims accuse 20 people of being witches and burn them at the stake.

1742: Handel writes *The Messiah.*

17th and 18th centuries: Scientists like Descartes, Pascal and Newton move to wean society off mysticism. Refuse to accept God on faith alone but resort to science to prove his existence. Spinoza claims the whole world runs on scientific principles: God is merely the sum of all the eternal laws that ever existed. Mendelssohn defines the path to God as moral conscience: people must rely on their own power, not the trappings of religious services.

1859: Darwin's *Origin of Species* published

1876: The telephone is invented. (Bell's conversation was not monitored for quality control.)

1878: The Salvation Army brings the light, and Thomas Edison turns on one of his own.

18th & 19th centuries: Philosophers like Marx, Hegel, Nietzsche and Freud maintain they have little use for God in their thinking. The English poet, William Blake, goes further: God is dead.

20th century: God is put to some difficult tests. How could the God of the Bible have stood by and merely observed the Holocaust? The God of the philosophers and the mystics had not performed up to expectation; the God of the Reformation and the Enlightenment had been witness to various annihilations in Europe and was seemingly indifferent. In the Muslim world, Ataturk changes Turkey to a secular state. To cap it all off, atheism now takes root. God's future seems in doubt.

By now you may have learned a thing or two you didn't know. On the other hand, you're puzzled why we even

went to the trouble to restate those chapters in capsule form. Here's our reason: in the next chapter, we're dealing with concepts of God which all have historical roots. That history is beautiful, interlocking, rich, violent, often convoluted, very long (very, very long) but always compelling and fascinating—and forms the "spine" of this book. Had we first presented this to you as we've just done, we would have not only done God an injustice, but the major players—and you as well. Thus this timeline to help you track the chronological flow of theology (the concepts or "classifications" of God) before you read about each of them in detail. Thank you for your indulgence. (And no, we're not selling them.)

CHAPTER 4

WHO OR WHAT
DO PEOPLE BELIEVE
GOD IS?

I n 1703, in the marsh country of Lincolnshire, England, a
mewling, underweight infant came into the world, the 15th
child of Samuel and Susanna Wesley. (Susanna herself was
the 24th of 25!) Following his education at Oxford and ordination, John Wesley began a revival movement in the staid Church
of England which eventually led to the 18th century equivalent
of a "contract" being put out on his life by the King's authorities. Undaunted, and after 250,000 miles on horseback and
50,000 sermons, the efforts of the little giant (5' 3", 123 pounds)
had created what would become the modem-day United Methodist church.

Four years after Susanna' s little "Jackie" saw the light of
day, Carl Linnaeus was born, the son of a Lutheran clergyman
in Sweden. After getting his medical degree, Linnaeus crossed
the Scandinavian peninsula 600 miles on foot to the Arctic
Ocean. His bent and genius eventually led him to publish a

workable survey of all the plants and animals then known to the world—7,700 species of plants and 4,400 animals.

This system, called taxonomy, became the underpinning of modem botany and zoology. It's why the grizzly is named *Ursus horribilis,* the dog *Canis famiiaris;* and we humans, *Homo sapiens*—or sentient being. That is to say, we're aware. We think. We reason. Sometimes.

Which brings us to the purpose of this chapter. We are going to try to classify the ways that God can be experienced. It may sound bodacious but I think it's important we go through this: think of it as on-the-job training—for both of us

A Taxonomy of God (Work in Progress)

1. **An anthropomorphic God:** one that takes a human form in the mind of the believer.

2. **A spiritual God:** a non-human form that can't really be seen but which can be experienced. (Sometimes referred to as a *theistic God* or *the God of scripture.*

3. **God surrogates:** A few extremely influential historical figures who, though not God, are "worshipped" by large numbers of people: Jesus, Mohammed and Buddha would certainly fall into this classification.

Moses also fell into this category up to and including the first century. But after the fall of the Temple, when rabbis replaced the institution of temple worship, these rabbis wanted nothing to do with that concept. Moses was then relegated into what is his current posture: that of a great servant/leader, visionary, man of wisdom and "bringer of the law." In other words, unlike the surrogate concept that still holds true for Buddha, Jesus and Mohammed, it does not hold true for Moses today. In fact, most Jews would be surprised to think of Moses in terms of "worshipping him," and unless I'm mistaken,

the idea would be anathema to Jewish orthodoxy. *Re-vered and honored,* yes—but not worshipped.

4. **A secular God:** A God that is neither anthropomorphic nor spiritual, but one that dwells in humans and manifests itself by the collective moral behavior of society.

5. **Variations and combinations of all the above.**

6. **The absence of God:** The concept of a supreme deity is either irrelevant, unimportant or rejected out of hand.

I think we're off to a good start, and I hope Dr. Linnaeus would concur. Please understand, however, our taxonomy is not the *only* taxonomy of God, and it has not received any theological stamp of approval, but consider the user benefits: it's straightforward, easy to understand and it will accommodate and classify all that I want to say on this subject.

Besides, I like it. It fits a book like this, which after all, was not written for theologians but for ordinary folk trying to sort out their feelings and who have no pressing need for something more involved and convoluted.

1.   The anthropomorphic God

We all know this one. (The first version in my memory bank must have come from my Mother.) God is...well, essentially an old white male, thin, tall, sharp facial features, has piercing blue eyes, an unruly mane of white hair, white flowing robe tied with a sash, and a wooden staff in his hands, all of which gives him a commanding aura. Sort of a thinner, less jolly Santa without the sleigh and the red suit and no Rudolph in tow. (Right up Hollywood's central casting alley.) Back then, he lived way "up there," and looked down over the parapet with his "X ray vision" and always knew what each of us was doing or thinking. (Of course, we thought Mom did, too.)

Many years later, my wife, Charlotte, and I with our three kids visited the Sistine Chapel at the Vatican. After entering the room, I looked up to see another version of my earliest God image, this one by Michelangelo. There was the anthropomorphic God, with a human form and face—the old white man from my childhood staring down at me, but now surrounded by angels, cherubs and golden harp. It's no wonder children grow up thinking of God in this manner. It seems so easy and natural. There's a hint of an eternal, benevolent and all-knowing Grandpa there.

Traditionally, then, that's the image we take from childhood into our teen years. Of course, there are millions of adults who still believe in anthro God. (We'll use this abbreviated version of what is a verbal mouthful.) Why would grown-ups believe in such a God? For openers, it's comfortable. We see old white men everyday so why can't one of them live in another place, converse with individuals and have significant power? Works for many. Then, too, our anthro God sidesteps a swamp of semantics and brain busting reasoning needed to put the pieces of the puzzle together: physiology, philosophy, spirituality and myth. It also fits neatly with the pictures and images of the God that we know. Anthro God is someone we can call up instantly on the picture tube in our head.

Question: Is anthro God functional? Does the concept fill the bill and fit the needs of those who believe in it? Most certainly. In fact, people not only tell us it does, but for the most part, their behavior suggests they are receiving sufficient moral direction from...*someone, somewhere.* They appear to be happy and satisfied with anthro God. Conclusion? It's functional. One issue comes to mind—how do they deal with the physical constraints inherent in anthro God? How does he go backward and forward in time faster than the speed of light? (Even a grandfatherly Clark Kent couldn't do that.) I would answer this by saying that if your belief is strong enough and the rewards are there, reconciling these physical constraints is a piece of cake. And like Sara Lee...nobody doesn't love cake.

2. The spirit God

This is the concept of God held by most Christians, Jews and Muslims. Unlike anthro God, spirit God can't be seen and has no form but is experienced. It is generally believed to be a God of heaven, but a God whose impact is strongly felt on earth. The idea of a spirit God (or Gods in this instance) was first written about by the Babylonians in their epic poem, *Enuma Elish,* which talked about a "mystery" and attempted to release its power. The spirituality in their writing is what's important here. At this point, it seems appropriate to pass on something said about spirituality by a very smart friend who said that "God gave humans spirituality and they screwed it up and turned it into religion." The monotheistic spirit God that the three major religions believe in today began as the Old Testament God, or the Hebrew God and, again, is referenced in Isaiah 45.21; "...there is no God apart from me." (That's about as plain as you can make it.)

The bump in the road came when I discovered that the Old Testament God didn't behave like the God of my early child-hood. (Or at least as he was presented to me then.) Old Testament God was powerful, brutal, murderous and volatile, though a kinder word might be inconsistent. He could change his mind in a flash. (Remind you of lightning?) For instance, after promising Adam he would die from the tree of Knowing and Good and Evil, God backed down and instead of death, imposed permanent sentences on Adam and Even—and the snake, too. This God saw the world's evildoing and caused everybody on earth to perish except Noah and his family....

The story of Noah was originally recorded in an earlier Babylonian narrative, the great *Epic of Gilgamesh.* There was a flood, and the fabulous Ark that contained all the creatures and so forth. Scholars generally believe that during the Babylonian captivity (6th century BCE) the Jews came across this account (written at least

1500 years earlier) and decided this was just what they needed to flesh out their early history. Don't despair or get the shakes: knowing this does not take anything away from the resonance, the charm, the power and the lesson to be learned from the Bible story as it's wonderfully told in Genesis. For a modern confirmation of the flood read *Noah's Flood* by Ryan and Pittman.

This is the same God, by the way, who allowed Cain to murder and go free, only to die at 70 from an arrow shot by his blind grandson, Lamech. (Hollywood screenwriters wouldn't touch that with a ten foot staff.) After the flood, having promised that he would never destroy the world again, God did destroy Sodom and Gomorrah over the pleadings of Abraham. His nephew, Lot, managed to get out of Dodge just in time, but his wife was turned into salt. This is also the same God who visited a harsh, punitive life upon the righteous man, Job, without ever explaining why. *(I am what I am...I do what I do.)* End of story.

In the first and second centuries, many who embraced the new Christianity rejected the God of the Old Testament, the cruel God of the Jews who had killed entire populations. People began to see Jesus and not the Torah as God's principal revealer. (If you feel the urge, flip back to the outline of the 3rd and 4th centuries CE.) Christians pondering over how God would be both one and three were told by Basil, *Epistle 38:4,* not to worry. Regarding Augustine and the Koran, we've already mapped that theological stream for you. And in the centuries yet to come, the eastern religions, chiefly Hindus and Buddhists, would give their take on a spiritual God. But let's zoom in on the end of the 6th century: by now the foundations of what we call the spirit God were firmly in place. People viewed this spirit God either as the one offering grace or as the "contractor" who promised that, if you do *this,* then I will do *that.* Peter Drucker, the well known management guru, is reported to have said this about grace: "I'm not sure how to define it, but it's the best deal in town."

3. God surrogates

The fancy word for this is *avatar*—in Hindu, a God coming down in bodily form to the earth. A handful of people we have touched on in our History of God have led exemplary lives, have been adored by their followers, have altered the course of history significantly, and consequently, have been raised to a level just below a deity—or maybe higher. Arguably, three prime candidates would be Jesus, Buddha and Mohammed. Of course, none of these ever claimed to be God, and in fact, all of them at one time or another made explicit statements to the contrary.

Despite their denying any claim to divinity, their words and actions had enormous impact upon others; thus, people followed them, loved them and "worshipped" them. Moreover, in the case of Jesus, many believed he *was* God. As it turned out, Jesus *(Yeshua,* in Hebrew) became part of the Trinity, and by implication, was blended into the alloy of a God of three parts or "persons." Accordingly, we've decided to choose Jesus as our example of a God surrogate: one who "stands in for God." Clearly, a large proportion of Christian religious activity is focused on Jesus and rightly so. God is never left out, but still, much of the liturgy, the music and the focus is on Jesus. Of late, this preoccupation has led to sloganeering, the latest of which surfaced about five years ago: "what would Jesus do?" (No mention of God.) Of course, it's easier to calculate what Jesus might do because we can relate to him as one human to another. He was not immune to the emotional spectrum that is part of our make-up. He shared a goblet of wine with the bar crowd, laughing at their jokes and stories, and as we have read, told a few himself. He wept in despair. He went ballistic at the desecration of the temple. He empathized with the marginal and brought healing to many who came to him believing. All in all, a man, but as Bruce Chilton has called him, clearly a "spirit person."

Of course, asking the question, "What would Jesus do?" cannot be posed in a vacuum. What would he do about what?

And when? The venal excesses of Wall Street? The degradation of crack street? The apathy on Main Street? The states' apparently inability to deal with child abuse? Would he storm into our posh country clubs swinging a nine iron? Would he show up on Sunday mornings at the finest churches—and be asked to leave? (The latter has been the subject of countless sermons, thus it's definitely on people's and pastors' minds.) The fact remains: he was there on the scene, larger than life; thus, it's easy for us to imagine him alive, though, and as we've commented earlier, the standardized portraits of him do leave much to be desired, A generation or two earlier, people took it on faith (oops) that the Jesus they saw on those little funeral parlor fans was the actual Jesus of history. Having said this, let's pose another question: as one embodiment of anthro God, does Jesus make it easier for people to believe in a spirit God?

That is a topic that seminarians could debate until.., hell freezes over. (I wasn't going to use that last construction, but somehow it fits.) Besides, I love the image it brings to mind. Imagine, Satan getting to run the world's biggest skating rink. Yes, it's absurd, but then some of what people have said about God and religion over the centuries has been equally absurd. More's the pity, it's led to a host of indignities, a litany of horrors that we've already treated; thus, a chuckle at this point is not only allowed—it's welcomed. Call it breathing room for the theologically challenged.

After Jesus died, much debate and deliberation ensued and seemingly without end. Everybody had a theory, every theory had a following, and every following had a falling out. The growing consensus for many was that Jesus had been more than just another man. Finally, after three centuries had passed, many took this further: not only had he been more than just a man, Jesus was God in human form. Today, many still have that same belief, regardless of what is in the dogma. One oft quoted line by eminent theologians who are also fervent believers and who feel the need to reconcile the two "sides" of this equation goes like this: "Jesus was never more divine than when he was human...and never more human than when he was divine." Some of you may regard this as a mere play on words; nonetheless, it has morphed into the longest running drama in history.

Now that we've examined and cross examined the facts and fables, I get to do my closing: do God surrogates make it easier for us—some of us—to believe in this being we call spirit God? I don't think there is any question that they do.

4. God as the collective conscience of the world (or at least, a smaller part of this world)

Except for some early references in Hindu mythology, this concept is more recent than the others we've talked about, and as far as we can determine, people haven't written books about it. But that doesn't mean they didn't think about it—in fact, a couple of them came close: Augustine said that God was a spiritual presence in everyone—he could have easily substituted the term "moral presence" but then who knows what was on his mind. Later, Mendelssohn did define the path to God as moral conscience and declared that people should rely on their own spiritual power and not the tinsel (did they have tinsel back then?) and trappings of religious power. No matter who, if anyone, gets the credit, all of the philosophers and mystics went down a lot of steep, winding paths in their journey toward the identity of God.

Instead of thinking of God as the collective conscience, what if we substitute collective "goodness"...or even "godliness?" After all, irrespective of their beliefs, most people think of godliness as our mirror image of what we think God is, or how he behaves. When (or if) you pray, clearly it's not necessary that everyone hear you. But if one purpose of prayer is to motivate people to demonstrate their innate goodness—a widely accepted assumption—then answered prayers are made evident via changed behavior, whether through individuals or groups.

Frequently, when some fundamentalist churches (and, incidentally, ultra Orthodox Jews) get together to worship, it's not unusual for the men to gather in a room and raise their voices in prayer, each one saying something different. And some believe that the man who prays the loudest has the best chance of his prayer being heard by God. We could say, then, that for those men in that room, faith is that God is hearing their prayers? Does God hear all of them at once? Can he separate each individual voice from the others? Is that faith based on spirituality? It would seem that without it, it's a hollow exercise in emotionalism or religious fervor. Perhaps it will help to think of spiritual belief like a copper cable that conducts the voltage of your faith. Sometimes 110, sometimes 220. Rarely 440.

The ESP (extra sensory perception) folks at Duke University have demonstrated that thought transfer is not hocus-pocus. Uri Geller, the Israeli psychic, once sat in a room, and observed by the British Royal Academy (or some other august and credible gathering) was able to bend a spoon by the power of his mind. If a human can do that, surely we can send a message through the ether. Is prayer, then, just another form of brain waves...spirit waves? And if we're not "sending" it to a spiritual God but a stone or a totem, then are we just playing theological Scrabble? I think it's safe to say that the collective conscience God is not a heavenly being, or a spiritual creation or an anthropomorphic form—rather, it's the inherent morality that resides in six billion plus people. The only problem is: some people are very moral, others are not. That's just the way things are.

Next question: do people who accept this concept of God believe their prayers are answered? Affirmative! Does their God act in response to requests or prayers? Clearly, they think so. I mean, if a tornado misses your community by the length of a football field, and you hear it said, "it was God's will," do you accept that? What about if, confronted by another kind of issue, you pray to that community's morality as God? Shouldn't you expect a similar favorable response? It's questions like these that have driven theologians half mad and led them to trundle down narrow stairs, candle in hand and tipple from wine casks in ancient cellars. The fact is: lots of people believe that both concepts are equally valid and attuned to our prayers.

Historians record that starting in the 11th century, the Crusaders felt divinely guided to embark on a killing spree the likes of which the world had never seen. *Divinely guided* That's hard to take, isn't it. I wonder who told them that. Apparently, some religious leader (was it Pope Innocent?) gave them a pep talk about how good their campaign of slaughter would make God feel. Is this the same God who protects their children and who provides food and shelter while they're gone? (I realize this is tough going here, for both of us, but we have to sort through this; however, let's take a more direct route.) Many of those who adhere to a collective conscience God don't think in terms of the entire world but rather the morality of smaller groups. And here's one example: How did 5th century priests who took the church to Ireland activate this morality in, say, a tiny seacoast village?

If a man stole a neighbor's cow or goat, some kind of punishment had to be administered. After all, stealing livestock was taking nourishment out of the mouths of helpless children. The problem for the priest was: if they imprisoned the man, or worse yet, killed him, his family would starve. That wouldn't work. They could banish him, but to where? And if they kept doing that, who would be left to attend church? Thus some ingenious priest came up with a plan. The miscreant would be brought down to the edge of the Irish sea one morning with all the village turned out to watch. He would then be made to wade out into the icy waters up to his waist and stand there for a time deemed to be sufficient by the priest, which sometimes would be hours. Finally, he

would be allowed back on shore to stand by a blazing fire and be rubbed and toweled until the shivers stopped. This punishment was given the name, *penance*. Afterwards, the priest would lead the community in prayer. It was a lesson to all that it was wrong to steal from your neighbor, a lesson that very few forgot. Best of all, the man was reunited with his family, brought back into "the community of faith" and allowed to resume his normal life. It didn't put an end to the stealing of livestock, but it did give potential wrongdoers pause to think about what *was* moral.

This is just one example of what we call "where-the-rubber-meets-the-road" religion. It helped to induce what theologians call orthopraxy or "right living" versus orthodoxy or "right thinking" which could be accomplished with mere words. Whatever term we use, the fact is, that within the dimensions of that paradigm, the collective morality of that small village became a force for good, for behavioral change, for a deepened sense of spirituality. The faith that was being expressed out there on that windswept shore was that moral behavior can be improved. Lessons can be learned. And stories about that day were told and remembered around countless campfires for hundreds of years (just as with the ancient Hebrews) while children listened, wide-eyed, trembling with the knowledge that God was more than a mystery and more than myth. God was somehow linked with the survival of that tiny band of believers. To them...God was real.

5.   Various combinations

"God is a spiritual force...a presence...something I feel...I just can't say more than that." The odds are you've heard one or more of these numerous times; therefore, it shouldn't surprise you to learn that this image of God has a large number of adherents. Its popularity comes from several forces. To begin with, the fact that those who believe it are unable to define it may well give it a curious spiritual aura. Like the God envisioned by early theologians, it's beyond our comprehension—unknowable by us ordinary mortals, but powerful nevertheless. A plus for many is that this kind of belief doesn't require a lot of heavy lifting. Since it's unknowable...well, why even try? In this manner, not only can you leave your brain in idle, the same goes for your imagination. Again, this is not new stuff: Symeon, the 10th century abbot, saw God in just this light—a mystery that could not be known.

The perks go on: if you're not inquisitive, who needs Bible study or (ugh) thinking? Believing in a non-anthro God doesn't alienate you from the spiritual sophisticates. You're not tagged with the atheist label; and best of all, this God can be explained with a no-brainer disclaimer: "For me, God is a spiritual presence, something I feel...I just can't say more than that." Not to offend some folks, all too often this image of God is used as the

SAM God: Socially Acceptable Minimum. It eliminates having to ask, or answer, questions. You avoid sounding stupid, and you'll never be confused. (Maybe with learning how to operate your new remote control, but not about God.) Is this God a genuine God? You bet. Does he hear prayer? He does if you believe he does. Does he respond? Mmm...you tell me.

"God is something, up there."

Boy, it's the "up there" part of this definition that drives me crazy. I mean, I thought the whole idea is that God is everywhere, so the "up there" business makes him less accessible to us. Of course, that explains why the scenario of the mystics was that we had to travel through seven heavens to get to God, which meant we had to go beyond "up there," to...well, God knows where! Does it make sense to you that the separation of God and humankind was an intended consequence? Many of the early philosophers believed that ordinary folk would never have a clue as to exactly who God was—that only scholars whose job it was to study these things, could figure it all out. So the "up there" thing was like a roadblock on the "highway to heaven." (That phrase was lit up in the church marquee in Robert DuVall's enchanting film, *The Apostle.)*

Okay. Enough of *up there.* Now what about the *something* part? That word opens the door to all kinds of images of God— actually, anything that will fit "up there" is fair game. But that's not new. God had quite succinctly defined himself to Moses as "I am who I am," and Acquinas shortened that to "he who is" which was brilliant editing. Of course, both of these leave a lot of wiggle room all the way from "God is something up there," to "God is a presence, a force...something I just feel, I can't say more than that."

That word *something* is a verbal non-starter. It sidesteps spirituality, shrugs off whether God is anthropomorphic, and shows a definite unwillingness to face up to the central issue, to wit: who or what is God? I mean, isn't that what we're really after here? I designed this book as a treasure hunt, not a search for trinkets. Thus, all of those vaporous, empty phrases and descriptions are...well, nondescript and leave us at the starting gate. And that's no way to run a race.

Variations and combinations, spiritually-based or not

Let's do the numbers: with 6 billion souls wandering around this hunk of clay, and a decent number searching for a God that fits who they are, it's a fair bet (remember, I wrote books on probability) that millions of conceptual variations of God are rattling around in people's brains. In fact, these concepts morph into other dimensions when groups of like-minded individuals get together, and believe me, there is no shortage of belief systems when you're talking about God.

Now take a look at some spirit God groups. You can find congregations of literalists whose T-shirts declare, "God did it, the Bible said it, and that's it."

Across town is another group that believes in a spiritual God, but not in the Jesus miracles. Down the street is yet another group that is not spiritually-based, has no liturgy but gets together for discussions about human behavior. And in the next town down the road you may find a *Urantia Book* study group. Participants from various denominations gather in private homes to discuss this 2097 page text, which exists in English and six other languages, and deals with subjects including the nature of God, the Trinity, universe cosmology, the history of the planet, and the life and teachings of Jesus. It is not a religion but rather a loose association. There are no doctrines or established dogma, only the teachings of the *Urantia Book* itself, which are subject to varying individual interpretations.

That's just for openers. Often the variations and combinations turn out to be extensions of the strong personality of a religious leader—perhaps one who became disaffected with the doctrine he/she had been practicing as with Smith and his Mormons. The leaders may be supportive or corrupting, but the one trait they share in common is their powers of persuasion. They create what we will call a "God of the intermediaries"—that is to say an individual god as interpreted by the leader. Jim Jones' suicidal group would be a tragic example of this. The Pilgrims who fled English persecution would be another. And then there was the group in California who were promised that their one way tickets would get them on a space ship and change in outer space for heaven. Should we laugh, weep, pray—all of the above? I'm never quite sure.

6. The absence of God

What follows is not—repeat, not a news alert. *Lots of people don't believe there is a God!* It doesn't matter what God we're talking about: mystic God, spirit God, collective conscience God, anthro God—no matter. They aren't buying it. And despite the fact that many religious leaders, along with their followers, are convinced that bad things will happen to these nonbelievers...I can't believe it's so. Most of them appear to live happy lives, accomplish good things, love their kids, recycle and drive safely. The ones I know personally do not consider "atheist" or "agnostic" as dirty words, and seem to shrug off the verbal barbs (and sometimes, bombs) sent special delivery by some of their God-believing brothers and sisters.

But what do they do for spirituality? By way of answer, here's a simple experiment you could perform: if you believe that one reason God gave you spirituality was so you could harness your energies for the common good of mankind, then follow your neighborhood (or family) atheist or agnostic around for a while and tote up the good things she does. If you get a long enough list, maybe that's your answer.

Wrap-up

There are several points worth noting here. First, no concept of God should either be accepted or rejected solely on the basis of whether it is spiritually based. Second, searching for a concept of God that holds all the answers is at best, an imperfect process—and at its worst, can turn out to be very frustrating. Some of these searchers get far too caught up in the process and have thus been described as being "so heavenly minded they're no earthly good." You obviously can't get around to trying all of them on for sighs, so you generally wind up adopting one that is nearest to what you need, or think you need, and then modifying it as you go along. More about how to do this in Chapter 12.

Finally, it's axiomatic that most people's needs change as they grow. What was appropriate for you when you were 5, is not likely to fit you when you are 35 or 85. Finding a God that fits you perfectly is like finding an off-the-rack suit that does likewise. As a young boy, my suit was generally a hand-me-down from my older brother. Mother wasn't about to spring for new duds for Dick. (Face it: who had any money?) She would make me try it on, this suffocating woolen tent that sagged and bulged, and I hated it, but Mom's favorite refrain was, "Don't worry, you'll grow into it." Are we supposed to grow into God? Is that the plan? Think about it, and we'll come back to this later on.

CHAPTER 5

WHY DO PEOPLE
NEED GOD?

I f that sounds to you like a stupid question, give me the benefit of the doubt and call it naïve. I haven't interviewed all those who say they need God. In fact, I haven't interviewed a hundred millionth of them (that's the number "1" with eight zeroes. But it's both effective and accurate in statistical sampling to draw inferences from a small sample of the population. Actually, the people with whom I've shared ideas about this book do constitute a fairly representative American sample. If you're in doubt about this, please consider that although there are 220 million TV viewers in the United States, only about 1200 TV sets are sampled to determine what programs our citizens watch. As I kept telling my students for 30 years, it really does work. Where I *am* on thin ice, however, is drawing the same conclusions about foreign cultures, Holy Rollers, 7th Day Adventists or Mormons whom I haven't yet sampled, chatted, discussed or in some cases, even visited. Well, what *are* the reasons people need God? We're going to examine about a dozen of these. Sure, there must be ten times that many, but in the interest of preserving forests, we have to draw the line somewhere.

Reason 1: To diffuse the fear of the unknown, especially the environment.

Let's time travel.., you're living in the year 5000 BCE. The sky opens up one day, and a bolt of lightning streaks down and turns your best bud into toast. Or perhaps it rained for five days straight and flooded out your cave or crops. Or the sky turned dark, a funnel cloud came down and you were suddenly missing a flock of sheep. Or an eclipse occurred and the sun seemed to be devoured a slice at a time. Most authorities now agree that an early concept of the Big Deity Up There became known as "El" the High God (or Sky God) of the Canaanites.

The worst part of this was: it was all beyond their control. Now, let's stay with that logic: if over time, you watched these things happen, with the resulting loss of crops, life and the like, you might just be moved to do something—anything—to placate the Great Whomever. Don't worry, we're not going to jump from here to prayer, but...the ancients did know how to connect the dots, and the dots said perform a ritual, and if you don't know one, then the best thing to do was to make one up. One thing led to another, and somebody, somewhere, someday performed a ceremony. And maybe something good happened. The rain stopped, the river receded, the wind died down, the disease went away, the enemy retreated, and the prototype of the first priest, preacher, rabbi, monk, shaman, imam (fill in the blank) hit a home run with the home town folks. I'm not saying this happened—I wasn't there. But just consider it.

Reason 2: To explain evil outcomes as "God's will."

If you live in the U.S. there's a good chance at one time or another, you've seen the bumper sticker, "shit happens." It's in mighty poor taste to display this publicly, but out of crudities like that come books such as *When Bad Things Happen To Good People.* Happens to groups, too, not just individuals. The Armenians, a religious group who comported themselves rather well in several countries, were decimated by the Turks in the 1920's.

Over 600,000 killed. A decade or so later, a demented World War I corporal, rejected as an art student, rose to power and all but "exterminated" (Hitler's word, not mine) the Jewish people living in Europe. If God is responsible for everything, as some claim, then how do we balance the books on such monstrous evil? Even after the fact, most of the rabbis continued to explain it away as God's will. I've always wondered what God's take on this was. My guess is that he was, and is, greatly offended.

DER

One final example: the sorry history of the treatment of African-Americans in the 18th to the 20th centuries. I won't catalog the cruelties that were visited upon them by their "masters," (including their tribal chiefs who, history informs us, sold them into slavery). Still today, many black church leaders explain their fate as God's will. I find it not only odd but singularly tragic that God gets the blame for all of the evil and violent outcomes that are not otherwise explainable, or not taken credit by other perpetrators.

The formula seems to be, if it's bad, blame God—and why not? It's quick, easy, convenient, and millions readily believe it. Best of all, God puts up no argument. And while we're on this subject, I would be remiss not to mention a slim volume called *The Will of God,* by Leslie Weatherhead. (Over a million sold, and still counting) Weatherhead separates will into three parts: (1) *Intentional* will—God's intent for us from the get-go. (2) *Circumstantial* will: I think of this as God's back-up plan when things go awry; and (3) *Ultimate* will: how God makes things wind up well in the end. At first, Weatherhead's thesis seems to make sense, but isn't he really saying that whether now or tomorrow, whatever happens, good or bad, comes under the umbrella of God's will. He gives himself a little breathing room with the concept of "circumstantial" which could be read as being in the wrong place at the wrong time. But God still calls all the shots, right? One would have thought that God would be a bit more discriminating or selective instead of merely indifferent. I don't know how all those million readers have reacted to this book (I'm sure the publishers are delighted) but they did buy it which means...they were searching for answers just like I am. And you?

Another fact of life is that the bad guys don't always get the punishment we think they deserve. In fact, Dame Fortune may smile upon them and they wind up fabulously rich and famous with long lives. You have to admit, it's a strange kind of bookkeeping, though some are quick to argue that God's credit ledger gets balanced over time. But then, that's not the point. Or is it? If I recall, God destroyed everyone but Noah and his family because the good/bad guy ledger was out of balance. Then afterwards when the flood waters had subsided, apparently evil cranked up all over again, playing catch-up (and as history has recorded, hasn't slowed down yet). Where do we go with that? You see the problem?

Reason 3: God is needed to explain good outcomes, too.

Your mother is diagnosed with a dread disease and given 90 days to live. She defies the odds and the experts and is still alive and healthy three years later. If a lot of praying had gone on, those who prayed would give God the credit. Not to do this would tend to make the whole issue of God's will irrelevant. At times with his children of Israel, God would be so disappointed, he would pitch a fit and punish them. Some say, "Well, God took it personally." But shouldn't it be in the very nature of God to take *everything* personally?

It's the same problem the ancients had with the elements: if you can't explain it medically and you're not comfortable with the statisticians' great escape hatch—randomness of outcomes and something called tails of probability distributions (don't ask; you don't want to know) then it's a lot easier all the way around to give God the credit. And nobody has yet said this is bad either!

Has the jury reached a verdict? I don't think so. Good things happen to bad people (the Mafia and a few crooked politicians are prime examples) and bad things happen to good people. A plane over Lockerbie, Scotland is blown up in mid air. We already mentioned the genocide in Armenia. Years later in 1988, a massive earthquake killed 55,000 Armenians in less time that it will take you to read this page. Is this adding insult to injury? Believers will wince and weep over this line and atheists shrug. All I can state with assurance is that philosophers, theologians and others have struggled with this for a very long time, with no end in sight. (Actually, if there *were* an end in sight, it would, as the finance guys say, cap it.) One final point to consider: Someone looks down and finds a twenty dollar bill, and a friend says to her, "You lucky devil." How is it that you never hear the phrase, "you lucky saint" or "you lucky angel or "you "lucky apostle?" I wish someone would explain that to me.

Reason 4:   15 million priests, rabbis, imams, ministers, sha-mans and other religious leaders need God as a jobs program.

Dick, you should be ashamed of yourself (Didn't I tell you the book would be slightly irreverent?) Granted, this may sound a bit cynical, but I'm dead serious...so let's do the math. There are 6 billion of us sacks of protoplasm sloshing if not slouching around the world. Using a SWAG, we can readily come up with how many of these belong to a religious congregation. (SWAG is one of those formal, academic terms used by erudite statisti-cians. It stands for sophisticated wild-ass guess.)

But let's look at the U.S. first—then we'll get to the rest of the world. The Gallup Poll (2001) tells us that there are 420,000 religious leaders in our nation. The estimate of average earn-ings is $40,000/year, which gives us a total annual remunera-tion of $14,408,000,000 (14.4 billion). And as they say in those tasteless TV offers, but wait, there's more. We have to add in the associated positions which include:

> Business manager-accountant
> Secretary
> Music director
> Adult education direction
> Youth activities director
> Associate pastor (rabbi, etc.)
> Custodian
> Others (web manager, drivers, organist, etc.)

Assumed ratio of associated positions to religious leader: 4.0
Assumed ratio of associate pay to religious leader's pay: .5
Total earnings for all religious positions in the U.S.
$14,408,000,000 + ($14,408,000,000 x 4.0 x .5) = $43,224,000,000
(43.22 billion dollars)

Mind you—that's per year, just for the United States. And now that your breathing has returned to normal, let's extend that for the whole world, by extending the Gallup Poll figures.

15 million congregations. (Estimated number of worldwide congregations)

Estimate of average earnings of religious leader: $25,000 annually

Total remuneration per year: $375 billion

Total earnings for all religious positions in the world:
$375,000,000,000 + (375,000,000,000 x 4.0 x .5) = $1,125,000,000,000 (1.12 trillion dollars)

Outfitted in their finery "with all FICA taxes paid, employer's share of the IRA" and benevolences (20%) the whole worldwide tab would come to about two trillion dollars a year! Hardly a cottage industry, wouldn't you agree?

Conclusion? Fifteen million people earn a living—some a very good living—by helping us find God! And that's not counting associated positions either. But don't get me wrong. I wouldn't diminish the net good of what all these people do; but what I am saying is that God is, in fact, the largest jobs program in the world. Here at home—and I would suppose abroad as well—many wear some kind of official regalia. Sometimes it's just a couple of suits, but these are hardly off the rack at Sam's Discount Suits. And in some cases there are robes hanging in the closets in the "pastor's study" (at least three). There are companies, big companies that make a handsome living off these and send out catalogs that would put the ritziest fashion designers to shame. Don't forget various and sundry stoles; the word for prayer shawl in Hebrew is *tallis* (rhymes with solace). Plus chalices, pew Bibles, hymnals, programs, organs, pianos, state-of-the-art sound systems...hey, the beat goes on, and the numbers keep going up. End of story.

All of which brings us to the ultimate question: Is there value in spending all that money? There must be, otherwise why would intelligent people do it? Besides, how would you ever fund unemployment benefits for 15 million people? Is that a kicker or what!

Reason 5: God makes people feel good.

No problem there. Being comfortable with your concept of God should make you feel good, even joyous. But that's really a modern concept. Some earlier theologians would—and did—take issue with this, claiming that God should be painful and devoid of joy. History records that some orders of monks would whip themselves with branches and briars until they bled (flagellation) as have the Shiites in Iraq recently. The practice was not uncommon. It hurts me even to think about it. On the up side, when you leave a worship service, there is every reason why you *should* feel good—about yourself, your relationship with God, about learning something new, expanding the dimensions of your understanding, about deciding to relate to someone else in a more positive way, about resolving to lend someone a helping hand, about how fortunate you are, about finding new meaning and purpose in your life...and about a hundred other things, too.

There are probably very few people who at one time or another have *not* experienced this warm feeling. And to that, I say hallelujah. (Write that down: It's only Chapter 5, and your author already said *hallelujah* twice!) But as to the source of this feeling, that's open to question. Some say it comes from spiritual proximity to God—reaching a harmony and balance. Others claim it evolves from the actual (spatial) proximity (after all, you have been in God's house). Still others attribute the inner glow to your having "gotten in touch with yourself" if only for a short time. Feeling good or joyous because of God is not, was not and *should not* be limited to a building or house of worship. I'm not about to start quoting you chapter and verse (I have to tread lightly here) but do check with your nearest, most knowledgeable and trustworthy source.

Some writers, with what the armed forces call "time in grade," state with considerable authority that the world would be a far better place if people's relationships with their God were entirely personal—heavy on the intimacy and light on the brick and mortar. And better still, if the institutions and trappings of organized religion (and, I assume, the 75 million leaders and associates who work there) were terminated. Gee, terminated is a harsh word. Laid off? Furloughed? Excused? You pick one.

Reason 6:   God provides protection and safety for all.

How did it go? *Now I lay me down to sleep, I pray the Lord my soul to keep. If I should die before I wake, I pray the Lord my soul to take.* Those words have been woven into the fabric of American life from time immemorial. Trust God to take care of you. If you just ask, God will take care of us, in life and in death.

My psychologist friends tell me that kids have strange demons. Children worry about things that go bump in the night; they seek protection from what they don't understand and comfort in knowing that someone is there (other than mommy or daddy) with the ultimate safety net. For most of us, this need, primal and pressing, does not vanish with age. It's part of the grain in our human lumber. As grown-ups, we still seek God's protection for ourselves and our loved ones. In hospital chapels, the prayers ask for healing. In airport chapels, people pray for a safe flight and a safe arrival. And in the old days, whaling ships, bound on a two-year voyage, caught a good wind and a rising tide out of the New Bedford docks—but only after prayers had been said for their safe return.

All right, let's take a closer look at this. Not a purely rationalist view, but a reasonable one. In the hospital scenario, why doesn't anyone ask for, say, the effective functioning of the anesthesia system? And in the airport, why not prayer for constant turbine pressure in the jet engines; and on the New Bedford docks, no one asked...wait a minute—maybe someone did pray that they would have fair winds and ride out the storms and the boat would not spring a leak. But you get the general drift. They all asked for God's blessing, in the form of a kind of protective umbrella. The implicit assumption therein was that something vital to their lives and livelihood was about to happen (this definition excludes football games though the livelihood of the coach—and players, too, if we're talking pro—is clearly on the line). The larger point is: it's a cry for help and an admission that there are forces at work out there over which we have no control.

Finally, a lot of people have no compunctions about whether or not they actually deserve this protection. The last act of a convicted serial killer before being executed is often...another prayer. I'm treading on thin ice here because the conventional wisdom is that it's never too late to seek forgiveness before your ticket is punched. But why wait until the last minute? Pardon the pun and the gridiron metaphor, but might this be a "hail Mary?" On the other hand, people are stubborn and hope springs eternal. There is a line in the Old Testament which may shed some light: "pray as if everything depended on God; work as if everything depended on you." That has always seemed to me to be a reasonable allocation of responsibility; and I would think it would go down with God equally well. But then, what do I know?

Reason 7: The capital markets need God, too.

We've already run the numbers on the "business of religion" but to underscore what we said, financing and running God's places of worship is one of the largest uses of capital in the world. Yeah, I hear what you're thinking: since most of the bucks are contributions, it isn't really an investment at all. Nonsense! You had a choice to buy IBM stock or invest in your house of worship, and you chose the latter. Anyway you slice that pie, it's still an investment, and who knows—the contribution may give you a greater return. Time out for another story break. Like all the others I use, this one is true.

In the early '90's, a certain pastor at a certain main line church in an upscale suburb north of Atlanta offered a "deal" to his members. He invited those who weren't tithing to start doing it for 90 days. If at the end of that period, their lives hadn't improved significantly, the church would refund their money. The point is: there were hundreds of "witnesses" to this money back offer, and well...you know how word travels. The offer was withdrawn after four months.

And while we're on the subject of money, here's another:

In the reign of Pope Leo X (early 16th century) indulgences were selling like hotcakes. This meant that if you had a deceased loved one who had sinned mightily and therefore, according to church dogma, was in purgatory, you could, in effect, buy that person's ticket out of hell and into heaven by purchasing an indulgence. A priest, Johannes Tetzel, was given the job of "sales manager" to get things rolling, and he came up with the first jingle in the history of religious marketing:

> *When the coin in the coffer rings,*
> *The soul from purgatory springs.*

Sales took off, the Pope was most pleased, and Brother Tetzel moved right on up the ecclesiastical ladder.

All right, we're back on track. But now apart from salaries, expenses, etc., there is the matter of assets. Accordingly, let's cipher a bit to see how much capital God's houses tie up. We'll stay with the number of 15 million congregations worldwide, but we'll define them in segments in order to get a fair estimate of the value.

Type	Approx. Cost	Approx. Number	Value
Mud hut	$1,000	600,000	$600 million
Basic one room wood	10,000	4,000,000	40 billion
Modest brick	50,000	4,000,000	200 billion
Large brick	200,000	5,000,000	1 trillion
Half a block brick	4,000,000	1,000,000	4 trillion
Mini cathedral	10,000,000	300,000	3 trillion
Modern cathedral	25,000,000	40,000	10 trillion
St. Peters, etc.	100,000,000	100	10 billion
		Approx. 15 million	

Total estimated value: $18 trillion, 250 billion, 600 million
In numbers: $18,250,600,000,000

I know—you're looking at that number and saying, "Dick, you gotta be kidding." I wish I were. However...I may have estimated my value on the low side. I mean, can you put up a fair to middlin' cathedral today for a hundred million? I think not. A decent synagogue that can seat 1000 people for high holy day services (the only time many Jews are seen inside) will cost $ 10-15 million. Just for kicks, let's double the cost to catch up with construction inflation, and our total is now $37 trillion dollars which is 50% larger than the gross national product of the world! Well, perhaps I made estimating errors in the way I broke up the 15 million buildings into categories. If this strains your credulity, let's cut the original number in half and we're down to a paltry $9 trillion dollars. The investment in religious buildings (forget furnishings, annual operating costs, etc.) is so gigantic, my brain can't handle it. First question: what could you do with $9 trillion in the way of education, health care, clothing and shelter? Change the world? Second question: what would *God* do with all that money? And with regard to those religious buildings—does He live in them?

Catholic scholar, John Dominic Crossan, has suggested that private houses be built with a "God Room" in them. This ingenious strategy of "worship decentralization" has the potential to save the world 9 trillion dollars.

Reason 8:   God offers a refuge from powerlessness, hunger and helplessness.

If you've never felt helpless or powerless or hungry, then you just haven't lived long enough. On the plus side of that, if you've ever attended a service in the Mormon Tabernacle when the choir hit 105 decibels...or the Ebenezer Street Baptist Church in Atlanta when the congregation starts to swing and reaches launch velocity, your heart quickens and your body picks up the vibes—if you have experienced this, then you've had a close encounter of the first kind—raw emotional power that is as elemental as the wind or the tides. You may be the least significant person on earth when you walk in the door, adrift in a sea of unconcern and totally without control over anything...but when that crescendo peaks, when the power surges, when the voltage slams through your spirit like a jolt of 220, you not only feel it, you become part of that power. An 8.5 on religion's Richter scale. There is nothing quite like it in the world!

Now, let's look at drawing on God's power cell from another perspective. Remember the old blues song that Bessie Smith made famous: *Nobody Knows You When You're Down and Out.* What do you do when you hit rock bottom? You ask God for help. The writer of the 23rd Psalm captured it perfectly: "Yea, though I walk through the valley of the shadow of death, I fear no evil...." There is the core of the power we're talking about.

It's a given you can whip all their asses if you have the biggest and boldest soldier of all lined up behind you. But you're no longer in the stands now. You've come down onto the field, and you're not a spectator—you're a player! Still another example. One of the enduring themes that screenwriters employ over and over is that of powerlessness. Remember, the classic film, *The Grapes Of Wrath?* The old model-T Ford breaks down, and there is the Joad family stranded five miles from nowhere— flat, stone broke with not even a dime for a gallon of gas. John Steinbeck wrote the dialogue that was as gritty as the Dust Bowl storms of the '30's, and director John Ford lifted us right out of our seats and into their lives. "How will we manage, Pa?" asks Henry Fonda. And the reply comes..."We'll just have to pray for help." Words and moments like this resonate deeply with us. We hurt because they hurt. We're all the walking wounded.

One final example of being the beneficiary of God's power. In the movie, *Chariots of Fire,* both of the finalist runners were deeply religious men—I should say, spiritual—one a Christian, the other a Jew. Both sprinters had considerable ability. And both of them asked their God to grant them some incremental power to win over the other. Furthermore, both were good and deserving men. This must have put a few more wrinkles in God's brow. What to do? In a lesser and lighter vein, this requisition for an advantage for both sides goes on every Fall Friday night at our high school football games. *Chariots of Fire* it's not, but to the people in the stands, don't tell them that. It's life or death!

Getting really serious, feeling helpless is more common than you might believe. Depression is the great destroyer of our time. Some so afflicted try to drown the hurt and rage in alcohol—others gobble down pills. Both options seem to work for the short term, with fleeting illusions of power, control, success and a grandeur that underneath is all glitz. But that road runs into a bridge and the bridge is out. On the other hand, seeking power from God is very natural, and the risk is near zero. Better still, it often works for many people. Psychiatrists state in that all-knowing manner of theirs that the help you get is all your own, i.e., if you're the fastest runner, you'll win the race. (Of course, you could stumble, and what then?) But the key is more than having the right physiology. It's *believing* you have it—and that's where God comes in. And now we've come full circle.

Reason 9: Some need God as a means of controlling mass behavior to achieve social, political and financial goals.

Back to the novelists again. (I keep going back to this because books speak a language that everyone understands.) In *Elmer Gantry,* God is used as the vehicle for separating poor people from their money. In more recent times, Jimmy Swaggart and Jim Bakker come to mind with their shameless con games; men like these rob, disappoint and worst of all, disillusion people about God. But as bad as they were, they didn't kill anybody. That kind of activity puts us into an entirely new league.

Actual destruction of life in God's name began 5000 years ago. The Babylonian gods fought among *themselves* for power and gave no quarter. The Romans destroyed the Temple of Jerusalem in the 1st century. The early 4th century saw the Emperor Constantine use God's power and the symbol of the Cross to wreak destruction on people whose beliefs didn't match his. Seven hundred years later, misguided Europeans massacred Muslims and Jews (and a lot of others they met along the way to the "Holy Land") and all in the name of God. We've already mentioned how Pope Innocent VIII used God and the power of the church to sponsor horrific witch hunts, persecution and torture, inflicting forcible baptism or expulsion upon Jews. Again...all in the name of God.

Even a theologian of the stature of Martin Luther used God to support his (Luther's) own deranged and displaced wrath against women, the poor and Jews, not to mention Papists and Anabaptists. In our own time, Shia and Sunni Muslims have turned their AK-47's on one another, both sides invoking (and no doubt vexing) Allah to bless their noble work. And who can forget the grisly photographs of Jim Jones serving a demonic communion by turning Kool-Aid into a deadly cocktail. Closer to home, al Qaeda fanatics invoke the name of Allah then destroy innocent life with a maniacal fervor that zaps our consciousness like a stun gun from hell.

There is no end to the accounts of people and groups who have used (and continue to use) God's name to achieve their monstrous goals. Unless I'm having a cerebral disconnect, I think that God has to be disappointed in these barbarians. At the same time, I think God is probably equally disappointed at the sheep-like behavior of those who allow it to go on. And we were supposed to be his finest work.

Reason 10: God provides an after-life.

Bishop James Thomas, born the son of sharecroppers in Orangeburg, S.C., was the first African-American bishop in the United Methodist Church. Once when he came to see the widow of a deceased friend, his greeting to her, delivered with a hug, was: "I'm sorry to hear about the death of your husband's *body.*"

Of all the creatures, man is the only one with any sense of the meaning of death (the end of life as we know it here on earth). Because of that knowledge, there has always been speculation on what happens after death, and indeed a lot of focus on whether there actually is an afterlife and if so, what's it like? How long does it last? Where exactly is it spent? And how can you be sure that you qualify? Some atheists and agnostics like to make the claim that God was created by man for that very reason, i.e., to provide the hope and expectation of such an afterlife. Heated debates over that have been going on for a very long time.

However, most people do believe in an afterlife—of some sort or other—and depend upon God to provide it. Maybe a better word is *guarantee* it. Turn on the news channel (or if you like words that stand still, pick up a newspaper). The suicide bombers who commit murder and mayhem in Israel are invariably shredded along with the victims, which defies all conventional wisdom. Military strategies never assumed that the enemy was willing to extinguish itself to win; the Japanese kamikaze pilots in WWII were, I believe, the one exception that comes to mind. Of course there were those Iranian kids sent into Iraqi mine fields to clear them.

But we must ask ourselves: what forces drive these young people to volunteer for these missions? They are predominantly men and they are promised that 70 (some say 72 but then, who's counting?) virgins await them in the highest level of Paradise. This promise is made to them by the Imams. Has God been hijacked? The answer is obvious. But remember—we're talking about people who *need* God, and in this case, they need God to make good on the guarantee.

Reason 11: God supplies a code of behavior.

Coming on the heels of the previous discussion, this thought seems grotesquely out of place, but let's follow where it leads. If you are an observant orthodox Jew, you adhere insofar as practicable, to the 613 *Mitzvot* (pronounced mitz-vote) rules or procedures proscribed in the Old Testament and elsewhere. They provide air-tight guidance for just about everything from birth to death, including the latter extremes. They establish dietary laws, rules for prayer, what to do about mildew, how to cut your hair, sex, and just about everything else. Clearly, you can do more—go beyond the boundaries—but you are forbidden to do less. Taken together, they offer a code of behavior with no room for ambiguity. Very few orthodox Jews think about behavior beyond what is written. If you just follow the *mitzvot,* everything will turn out all right. Think of them as the lines on a tennis court. The ball is either in or out. If it's out, ostensibly one hears the judgment call... *"fault!"*

Rabbis point out that these 613 laws were set down by intelligent men at a time when life was fragile—when support systems did not exist. No family guidance counselors were around. Nor were medical research and health delivery systems. It was a time when social relationships and societal order needed constraints—baselines, plus a net. And as such, they served as a kind of "How To Guide" for life and survival—certainly a vital function. Moreover, it is fascinating to observe that many of them still have considerable practical value even today.

Going from the Torah to the Koran, we find a somewhat similar prescription for behavior, but it doesn't come pre-assembled in 613 working parts. Interestingly, when you read the literature of any religion, you find a code of behavior of one kind or another; and, if you believe that God is a behaviorist, this shouldn't surprise you. For the record, let me state that I don't believe that everyone looks to God (or should look to God) to be told where and when to make every right and left turn on the road of morality. No, I don't believe that for a minute. But...I can't help but notice how a surprising number of people have...well, subcontracted to God the responsibility for doing their individual and in some cases group thinking on behavior. Helping your kids with homework is okay. Doing it for them is not.

Finally, let's look at the New Testament and see if we can find a counterpart to what we've cited from Torah and the Koran. In Matthew 22:37-40, we come across Jesus in a debate with an "expert in the law," who asks him "Rabbi, what is the greatest commandment in the law?" Jesus gives him the answer, "love the Lord your God with all your heart, all your soul and all your mind." Of course, Jesus knows he is quoting directly from Deuteronomy 6:5 (which brings us right back to Torah). He tells the Pharisee this is the "first and greatest commandment," then goes on to add, "and the second is like it: love your neighbor as thyself." But his final words are the ones that cap the debate: "all the Law hangs on these two commandments." Old Testament, New Testament and the Koran: three sources, three interpretations, three prescriptive codes of behavior as to how God intended for us to live. But the current that runs through all of these flows from the same headwaters—one God.

Reason 12: Some folks in the "null set" need God.

I've always liked that term and thought it never got its due. (There was even a coffee house in the 60's in Durham, North Carolina, called the Null and Void. Nobody knew from nothing about latte then.) In mathematics, the null set means "where everything else isn't." Take religion as an example. If we say that 95% of people believe in God, then the null set would be the remaining 5%. We know what's in the 95%, but what's in the null set? In my North Carolina hometown—little, southern and country to the core, the words atheist and agnostic were rarely spoken and in many places this practice hasn't changed much. Just because atheists believe there is no God and agnostics question the existence of God in the absence of material proof, this doesn't mean they have horns...speaking of horns, I have something to say here....

In the Sistine Chapel sits Michelangelo's famous statue of Moses. Cameras click because this Moses has horns. Horns? How can that be? The reason is that in the late 4th century (CE) Pope Damasus sent Father Jerome to translate the Hebrew texts into Latin (the Vulgate) and where the Old Testament said "rays of light issued from Moses' face," Jerome mistranslated "rays" to "horns." There's more: Michelangelo was aware of the mistranslation but put on horns anyway. Though appropriate to a satyr, they hardly fit the man whom God had called up on Mt. Sinai to receive the Law. Tragically, the myth of Jews with horns was popularized during the Dark Ages that followed. Today, the cameras go click, and the false image is indelibly etched in the minds of millions. Thus is history writ large—and wrong.

Back to atheists and agnostics. They don't have horns or webbed feet nor are they prohibited from voting. It's just that they don't believe in some things that the other 95% tell us *they* do. I wonder—where would the atheists and agnostics be without God? Now that would present a real problem, because the absence of God would mean that they were no longer the null set but the "main" set.

But I'm not going to pick on the atheists, or agnostics. I made a promise up front that I am not in the "club bashing" business and I meant it. There are lots of others in the null set who need God in order to justify what they do. (Apparently, a couple of them work for *The New Yorker* magazine as cartoonists.) Lots of readers have both chuckled and groused over those cartoons that may show two people discussing the presence or absence or the meaning of God. I for one would hate to see that disappear.

And let's not forget the "soap box" guys on New York's Time Square who give their take on God with enormous enthusiasm and from every imaginable point of the theological compass. I would be quite concerned to see those in the null set on those corners move to the unemployment line. Okay, enough. If you think I have my tongue way out in my cheek, you're right! But my point—and I do have one—is that God is used as a "whipping boy" for lots of folks. Thankfully, we live in a nation that allows them (and me) to get on with our philosophizing and foolishness.

Wrap-up

I promised you a dozen examples of why people need God, and that's all she wrote—for this chapter and this book. Peggy Lee used to sing the question, "is that all there is?" No way. There are about 11,000 books on God, and probably a hundred new ones written each year. If the thought of that overwhelms you, what would you rather all those authors wrote about? Sex? Statistics?

Heaven forbid!

CHAPTER 6

WHAT DO PEOPLE BELIEVE ABOUT GOD?

That's a very important question in a book like this, and you could legitimately ask why we waited this long to answer this. In fact, we didn't wait, but actually started answering it way back at the start of Chapter 2. We approached the question historically by sifting through what various groups believed about God at various points in history. Chapters 2 and 3 then reviewed God beliefs from 15,000 BCE up through the 20th century. In light of this: your question is valid. Why do we need a complete chapter now on what people believe about God?

I like good questions, and here's my answer. Scholars, which I am not, would use a fancy word to address this question. They'd point out that an historical review is called a longitudinal study—*longitude* in this sense meaning across time. Such studies are helpful in teaching us how things like values, beliefs and customs change over time. But we want to cut into this very long time line at some point and do an in-depth examination of what exactly is going on, we'd call that a *latitudinal* study.

In magazine publishing, the terms vertical and horizontal media are used. *Newsweek* or *Time* would be an example of horizontal media, targeting a broad audience, whereas *Engineering Week* or *Aeronautical News* would be vertical media—probing one specific area of interest in great depth.

Now back in the fourth grade, some of my classmates got longitude and latitude mixed up, but what impressed everyone was how this science enabled mariners to sail around the world, and this was before the advent of Global Positioning Satellite technology. All right, let me hoist sail and get back to the beginning. What you and I did in Chapters 2 and 3 was to sail east to west (or west to east) crossing thousands of years of history (longitude lines). And what we're getting ready to do now is stop and sail north and south along a single longitudinal line, which we could call "now." Because we're going to examine what people believe about God right now, not in 2000 BCE or 300 CE or in 1986—but right now! And when we've finally docked, we should have a decent idea of current beliefs about God and related topics.

One final technical note about sailing. While we're sailing up and down the "now" longitudinal line, we may throw in some data from a couple of other such lines to show how things may have changed. Of course, by now you're such an expert on research and marine navigation, you will quickly recognize this as *throwing in a few longitudinal excursions in our latitudinal study.* Right? O.K., let's cast off all lines!

Religions of the world

10,000 and counting

Hard to believe, isn't it? Ten thousand religions 150 of which have at least a million followers. Within Christianity alone, there are 33,830 denominations—from the largest, Catholicism, to the smallest, the Shakers. For those of you who enjoy keeping score, here's a rough and ready tote board of what are generally recognized as the principal belief systems regarding God.

Religion	World Adherents
Christianity	1,943,038,000
Islam	1,300,000,000
Hinduism	900,000,000
Secular/Nonreligious	
Agnostic, Atheist	850,000,000
Buddhism	360,000,000
Chinese traditional	225,000,000
Primal-indigenous	150,000,000
African traditional	
& Diasporic	95,000,000
Sikhism	23,000,000
Juche	19,000,000
Judaism	15,000,000
Spiritism	14,000,000
Baha'i	6,000,000
Jainism	4,000,000
Shinto	4,000,000
Cao Dai	3,000,000
Tenrikyo	2,400,000
Neo-Paganism	1,000,000
Unitarian-Universalism	800,000
Rastafarianism	700,000
Scientology	600,000
Zoroastrianism	150,000

(Christianity includes Catholic, Protestant, Eastern Orthodox, Pentecostal, Latter Day Saints and Jehovah's Witnesses. Numbers tend toward the high end of reasonable worldwide estimates but relative order is accurate.)

The Harris Polls of Beliefs of U.S. Adults, 1994,1998,2000 and 2003

These are perhaps the best continuing studies of U.S. religious beliefs. If you're wondering, typically, they survey between 1000 and 2000 adults by telephone to produce statistically significant results. Here are the results of the 4 such Harris polls.

	1994	1998	2000	2003
Believe in God	95%	94%	94%	90%
Believe in heaven	90%	89%	89%	82%
Believe in divine miracles	81%	86%	85%	72%
Believe in hell	71%	73%	73%	69%
Believe in the virgin birth	78%	83%	82%	77%
Believe in the resurrection	87%	88%	86%	80%

Conclusions: Over nine years the data are relatively stable with a slight downward trend. In general, levels of belief are higher among women, African-Americans and people with no college education.

Of the 90% who believe in God, women slightly outnumber men.

Of the 82% who believe in heaven, 9 out of 10 are women and among men, 3 out of 4. The 82% who believe in heaven falls to 71% among people 25-29 and those with postgraduate degrees.

Of people who call themselves Christians, 1% do not believe in God, 7% do not believe in miracles, 5% do not believe in heaven and roughly 1 out of 5 do not believe in hell.

Even more surprising—26% of those surveyed who say they are *not* Christians believe in the resurrection of Jesus and almost the same number in the virgin birth.

The Gallup Polls on Creation

These are results gathered from 17 years of polling to find out which of the following four positions people took on the subject of creation, always a controversial topic.

God created man pretty much in his present form at one time during the last 10,000 years.

Man has developed over millions of years from less advanced forms of life, but God guided this process including man's creation.

Man has developed over millions of years from less advanced forms of life and without the help of God.

No opinion

	1982	**1991**	**1993**	**1997**	**1999**
Creation by God at one time in last 10,000 years.	44%	47%	47%	44%	47%
Man developed over millions of years with God's guidance (including his creation)	38%	40%	35%	39%	40%
Man developed over millions of years without God's participation	9%	9%	11%	10%	9%
No opinion	9%	4%	7%	7%	4%

Two interesting conclusions. (1) With regard to the first three positions, beliefs have held relatively stable over this 17 year period. (2) But the proportion of those who say they have no opinion has fluctuated and fallen.

Is God a he or a she or...? In 1997, an ABC News survey found that 44% of those interviewed believed that God was a man. Just about as many said God had no gen-

der, while only 1% thought God was a woman. 12% couldn't make up their mind.

Believers and nonbelievers

A demographic snapshot

Some of the best surveys available were taken by the National Opinion Research Center. The data are the combined results of studies in 1988, 1991, 1993 and 1998.

For the purposes of this study, *belief* includes the following four views:

I know God exists, and I have no doubt about it.

Though I have doubts, I do believe in God.

I believe in God some of the time but not all of the time.

I don't believe in a personal God but I believe in some kind of higher power.

Disbelief has two definitions

I don't know whether there is a God, and I don't believe there is any way to find out.

I don't believe in God

	Believe in God (93+ %)	Do Not Believe In God (6+%)
Gender		
Male	42%	63%
Female	58%	37%
	100%	100%
Age		
18-29	20%	25%
30-39	24%	27%
40-49	19%	20%
50-59	13%	11%
60+	24%	17%
	100%	100%
Education		
Less than high school	21%	14%
HS graduate	31%	22%
Some college	25%	24%
College grad.	13%	20%
Post grad.	10%	20%
	100%	100%

Conclusions:

Gender-wise, almost twice as many males as females do not believe in God.

Age-wise, in the 50-59 segment, the numbers fall sharply with regard *to both belief as well as non-belief* Could this be the fallout of mid-life crisis or what? I'm not sure, and I don't think anyone else is either.

With regard to education, the percentage of high school graduates who believe in God is three times that of post college graduates. Conversely, between these same segments there is a 100% increase among postgraduates, telling pollsters they do not believe in God.

Looking at born-again Christians and non-Christians

Prepare thyself to be surprised

George Barna is one of the most widely-known and respected researchers whose focus has been on behavioral aspects of the church. This born-again Christian sociologist has made it his business to examine religious beliefs, views and values of our society, and in his book, *The Second Coming of the Word,* Barna reports his findings as gathered through a series of 12 questions. I think even the most casual reader, despite your religious views, will find these fascinating.

	Born-again Christians	Non Christians
Have been divorced	27%	23%
Gave money to a homeless or poor person in the past year	24%	34%
Took drugs prescribed for depression in the last year	7%	8%
Watched an X-rated movie in the past 3 months	9%	16%
Donated any money to a non-profit organization in past month	47%	48%
Bought a lottery ticket during the past week	23%	27%
Attended a community meeting on a local issue in the past year.	37%	42%
Feel completely or very successful in life	58%	49%
Impossible to get ahead because of financial debt	33%	39%
Still trying to figure out the purpose of your life	36%	47%
Currently satisfied with the way your life is going	69%	68%
Personal financial situation is getting better	27%	28%

Conclusions

As we said at the outset, much to our surprise, whether one is a born-again Christian or a non-Christian, with a few exceptions, in most cases the differences are slight. Ironically, 1 of 3 non-Christians reported giving money to a homeless or poor person compared with 1 of 4 born-again Christians. Also surprising, born-again Christians are slightly more likely to be divorced than the other side. Regarding renting an X-rated movie, almost twice as many non-Christians as those born-again were likely to indulge themselves. If someone other than George Barna had done this study, some quarters might be tempted to look at it askance, but his credentials are solid, and if there were bias involved—which there is not—it would surely favor the "other side." Make of these what you will, but the findings are, at the least, most interesting.

Edison Media American Religious Preference Survey, 2002

A revealing snapshot

Four questions were asked:

How important is religion in your life?

How often have you experienced God's presence (or the presence of a spiritual force that felt close to you)?

Is the religion you practice the only true religion or do all religions have elements of truth in them?

Is the most important part of religion doctrines beliefs or individual experience?

Recap

Nine out of ten people find religion to be very important or at least somewhat important.

One of every two people report having had a "spiritual encounter" many times. One out of five say, "several times."

Four out of five people say all religions contain elements of truth.

Nearly 3 times as many people rate individual experience as being more important than doctrines or beliefs.

World's religious profile by geographical regions

The Gallup International Millennium Survey (2002) was conducted in 60 countries which together represent one fifth of the world's population. The data were grouped in the following 6 geographical regions. The first question asked was: Do you belong to any religious denomination?

West Africa	99%
Latin America	96%
North America	91%
Western Europe	88%
Eastern Europe	84%
Southeast Asia	77%

Recap

Almost 9 out of 10 belong to some religion

West Africa's high score may reflect a high incidence of Muslims and where Catholicism has made large inroads in recent years.

Interestingly, in Hong Kong, 2 out of 3 people do not belong to any religion. (At least, that's what they tell the pollsters.)

Comparable figures for the Czech Republic and South Korea were 55% and 45% respectively.

When the second question was asked, "Do you attend religious services regularly," the results changed as follows:

West Africa	82%
North America	47%
Latin America	35%
Western Europe	20%
Eastern Europe	15%
Southeast Asia	4%

Recap

On average, 32% say they attend regularly, 35% say "every now and then, and 33% answer "never" or "less than once a year."

Women attend more regularly than men (35% against 28%).

And people with only a primary education attend more than others (33% to 25%).

On the question, "How important is God in your life?," people responded on a scale of 1-10 with 10 being very important. The results were then converted to percentages.

West Africa	97%
Latin America	87%
North America	83%
Eastern Europe	49%
Western Europe	49%
Southeast Asia	47%

Recap

Essentially, people's religious beliefs are not primarily given voice through religious institutions or established worship services but rather as a personal prayer or meditation relationship directly with God.

The poll also asked respondents what their image of God was. Almost half said they thought of God as a person, while 30% saw God as a spirit or life force, and 14% didn't think there was any spirit, God or life force. In terms of the 6 research regions, here are the results:

	Personal God	Spirit/ Life Force	Neither Spirit, God Nor Life Force
Latin America	64%	24%	3%
North America	62%	29%	2%
Southeast Asia	27%	29%	11%
West Africa	61%	31%	4%
Eastern Europe	42%	29%	9%
Western Europe	35%	36%	15%

Recap

More women than men see God as a person, but the genders are equal in terms of those who see God as a life force.

Men are more likely to deny God's existence.

The elderly are more prone to see God as a person as are those with less education.

The prevailing image of God as a person is almost the same in Latin America, North America and West Africa.

It's the elderly and the less educated who believe there is one and only one true religion; and geographically, they are concentrated in West Africa and Latin America.

Finally, the Gallup Poll gave respondents a choice among whether there was (1) one and only one true religion, (2) many true religions or (3) no true religion. Results were these:

	One True Religion	Many True Religions	No True Religion
Latin America	48%	35%	11%
North America	20%	71%	6%
Southeast Asia	31%	38%	11%
West Africa	62%	31%	2%
Eastern Europe	30%	34%	11%
Western Europe	21%	55%	17%

Scientists and religious belief

In 1914 and 1933, James Leuba mailed a questionnaire to a sample of 400 *American Men of Science* leading scientists, asking about their belief in God and in immortality. He got a 70% return rate in 1914 and 78% in 1933. In 1998, Edward J. Larson and Larry Witham sent a questionnaire with the same wording to 517 members of the U.S. National Academy of Sciences. The return rate was slightly over 50%. Here are the results which reveal some fascinating changes in attitudes and mind-set.

	1914	1933	1998
Do you personally believe in God?	27.7%	15.0%	7.0%
Do you personally disbelieve in God?	52.7%	68.0%	72.2%

Do you personally believe in immortality?	35.2%	18.0%	7.9%
Do you personally disbelieve in immortality?	25.5%	53.0%	76.7%

Recap

By 1998, personal belief in God among scientists declined to one fourth of what it had been at the start of WWI.

Belief in an afterlife declined even more dramatically.

And personal disbelief in an afterlife *tripled!*

In September, 1999, *Scientific American* reported that whereas over 90% of the general U.S. population has a distinct belief in a personal God and life after death, only 40% of scientists with a B.S. degree share this same view. And only 10% of those who are considered eminent scientists believe in a personal God or an afterlife.

A 1998 survey of members of the National Academy of Sciences revealed that 3 out of 4 respondents were atheists, 21% agnostics (unsure or silent about God), and only 7% admit to a belief in a personal God.

Finally, in July 1998, the journal, *Skeptic,* (Vol. 6, No. 2) published the results of a study that compared professions and the likelihood of belief in God. Whereas the general population was slightly over 90% likely to believe in God, scientists and mathematicians in general were only 40% likely, biologists, 30% likely and physicists only 20% likely to believe in God.

Wrap-up

It would be redundant to restate what you've already read. If some of you felt slightly overwhelmed by my tables, I apologize. This was just by way of wanting to assure you that I did my homework.

The conclusions? Admittedly, these are broad, but so is the subject matter.

Most humans believe in God, but then, when such a question is put to people, it is not surprising that they would answer in the affirmative. People also believe in the presence of oxygen in our atmosphere—without which we could not exist—but few seem to get very excited about it. The more relevant question should go like so: does this belief significantly shape your behavior and, therefore, your life?

Over time, the changes that one's belief in God undergoes are not dramatic but tend to be only slight shifts in tone and intensity..

Belief in God does vary significantly throughout the world.

Finally, scientists are a special case, especially physicists and mathematicians. Which brings us to the most famous of the latter group—Albert Einstein, a strong believer in order in the universe whom we have chosen to give the last word. (Quoted from *His Life and Times*)

"I shall never believe that God plays dice with the universe."
"It is the purpose of science to explain the mystical."
"All I want to know is "how God did it; the rest is detail."

CHAPTER 7

FAITH IN GOD AND FAITH IN YOURSELF

Faith as one's religion

F aith is loaded with all kinds of meanings. So let's begin with faith defined simply as one's religion—or denomination. And here in the South, it has long been a way of defining oneself. When people meet, one of the first questions generally asked is, "What church do you attend?" (This supplants the urbanized Yankee version: "What line are you in?") And when someone replies, Baptist, it means that individual accepts the doctrines that attend the Baptist segment of Christianity. Of course, that gets us into exactly *which* Baptist segment, and that road can split off into several others. So we'll exit there.

If you'll pick up your phone directory and thumb in the white business pages to the listing "Faith," you'll probably find a few churches. Perhaps even an enterprise that's a spin off from a church, Faith Child Care or Faith Rescue Mission. In addition, there are websites called God, Inc., the Church of God by Faith, Inc., and

Faith, Inc. But what you *won't* find is Faith Used Cars, Faith Insurance Agency or Faith Stockbrokers (my vote for oxymoron of the year). In general, people tread lightly with using that word, other than for churches, a girl's name and a few gospel groups. But not for business.

Back to our Baptist friend. Her church orientation or identity as a Baptist means she has definite ideas, doctrinal and otherwise, about religion. Divorce and baptism come to mind first. For her, the latter would mean total immersion, which, interestingly enough, it did for the Jews in the time of Jesus. When Jesus went to the banks of the Jordan, he met John the Baptizer (that's his right name, not John the Baptist, and no, he didn't found the Baptist church). At that time, those Jews too poor to have their own ritual bath, called a *mikvah*—we're talking about 98% of the population—had John dunk them in the muddy waters of the Jordan, thus signifying they were ready to worship God. Fast forwarding, Methodists sprinkle, Baptists dunk. And never the twain shall meet.

If you are a Baptist—make that a Southern Baptist—chances are you won't change your beliefs. Of course, marriage might make a difference or if fault lines cause a family quake. And it's not unusual for a Baptist church to split, some of the congregation leaving to start a new one just up the road. My younger brother lives in rural upstate South Carolina, and he reports there is a Mt. Blank (we'll keep it anonymous) Baptist Church, (a large one), then just a half mile away, New Mt. Blank Baptist Church (smaller) and then down the road a piece, New Reformed Mt. Blank Baptist (smaller still). You get the idea.

Interestingly, many Jews who lived in the rural south found themselves hundreds of miles from other Jews and far from the nearest synagogue. One result of this was their marriage to non-Jews, yet another example of one partner likely to change faith. I'm wandering a bit, but this is fascinating stuff, and besides, we're having fun. (See, if you were a Puritan, you'd have a problem with this.)

A lot of people in various denominations or faiths experiment. Consultants who get paid to know about things like this call it "church shopping." In marketing, we call it *brand switching,* like moving from Crest to Close-up. A surprising amount of this goes on, in part motivated by the increasing budgets for church promotion and advertising. More and more religious leaders are aware of what is called "the graying of the pews" (aging congregations) and are casting the net for young couples, and offering them attractive programs to maintain church membership. By the way, none of this has very much if anything to do with faith. Now we're talking what is called in the rural south, *bidnis.*

Faith as belief in oneself

This is a belief system based upon an honest inventory of one's own strengths, skills and talents. A few quick examples should suffice: if you're the best bricklayer (mason with a small "m") in town, your confidence—or we can call that faith—in your skills allows you to tackle any job that comes your way. If you're on a job interview in another town, you may have a lot of *faith* in your ability to impress your new potential employer. A good hitter steps into the batter's box with the faith he's going to get a hit. On his best day, maybe even a homer. Now, the question. Can this kind of faith be enhanced by faith in God? Sure it can. But without faith in your strength, your determination, your commitment to goals, to family, to right living, God won't have very much to work with. But then, he's seen all this before. (We'll talk more about this later.)

Welcome to the Bible Hall of Fame. Ring a bell? No? Then what about a Hall of Faith? Ah hah, there we're on more solid ground; accordingly, if we thumb to the book of Hebrews which, of course, was never intended to be a book but merely a letter. A letter written by

whom? Well, scholars are not sure. Maybe Barnabas, maybe Apollos, but certainly not Paul. Anyway, in Chapter 11, the writer lauds a number of Old Testament personages and patriarchs—Enoch, Abraham, Moses, Joseph and others—telling us they lived and walked by faith, thus their being singled out for special mention. My favorite verse (wow. I never thought I'd hear myself saying those words) is 11:31, "By faith, the prostitute, Rahab, because she welcomed the spies, was not killed...." Surprise! Hardly a luminary and certainly not a patriarch, nonetheless, Rahab, our lady of the evening, winds up in some pretty good company, and all because of her faith. (I guess you could say she wound up in the hall of fame after all.)

Faith in a spiritual God

Belief and transcendence

Strong and consistent belief in a spiritual God is not the easiest thing to do. Yet, in my conversations, some people have told me it's very natural for them. It's simple. And it doesn't take a lot of thought. I wonder. Let's look at the record: over the 7,000 year history we've reviewed, God has not been particularly easy to stick with. In fact, in many cases, God has behaved inconsistently. We've already discussed some of these in the Garden of Eden story, those in the murder of Abel, and those arising from the fate of Sodom and Gomorrah. In each instance, God promised one thing—yet *did another.* If you're a student of the Bible, you're no doubt familiar with other similar examples where God's behavior changed without explanation...that is, *apparent* explanation. After all, God himself made it very clear that "he was what he was and that was it." In essence, take it or leave it, said the Old Testament God. Centuries later, the writer of Hebrews would help his readers come at faith yet another way. It was, he said, "the assurance of things hoped for—the conviction of things not seen."

There is another question we have to deal with—one of the time lag between God's promises (or threats) and these actually being carried out. Let's look at how the writer of the book of Job crafts his scenario. Satan tells God that Job is acting faithful only for what he can get out of it. God allows Satan to put this to the test, and while losing everything, Job's confidence remains rock solid. More suffering takes place, particularly the loss of loved ones, but Job still hangs in there. His friends tell him he must have sinned to deserve this punishment, but God finally sets the record straight: I will punish whomever I want and when I want and I don't have to give a reason. Job finally comes to understand it was his pride that led him to think he could factor God into a cause-and-effect equation, but he realizes he was wrong and apologizes. God restores him to his former happy state. End of story.

I couldn't have stuck it out like Job. At least, I don't think so. And I wonder how many readers share my position. Here's another take, this one in real world terms. Many years ago, my older daughter and her friend simultaneously came down with severe strep throat. The parents of my daughter's friend were Christian Scientists who are prohibited from seeking help from medical professionals (with some notable exceptions). Upon confirmation, my daughter's physician started her on antibiotics. The mother of my daughter's friend rejected medicine, telling us they would rely upon prayer. Both girls recovered, but then, that wasn't my point. I was stunned by their depth of faith, despite the potential danger facing their child. I have to tell you that absolutely awes me. If that's not putting your life in your faith, then I don't know what is.

There's more. In 1993, a physician, Larry Dorsey, published a book, *Healing Words: The Power of Prayer and the Practice of Medicine.* In its pages, he reported the results of 131 controlled trials of healing attributed to prayer; 56 of these demonstrated "statistically significant" results. In plain language, the relationship between prayer and healing in these 56 cases *could not have happened by chance.* Both instances, my daughter's friend and these clinical studies, make a convincing case for a lot of people. (Maybe you're one of them.)

Generic faith

Learning from the pattern of performance

We could call this secular faith to separate it from faith in God, and by this we mean a strong belief that something specific will or won't happen. It's related to faith in oneself, but often it is a level of trust that generates its strength from a source we don't fully understand. You've heard people say, "I don't know why, but I just know that's going to happen," and they're not basing that on anything specific from within. Now comes the follow-up. Is it possible to have this kind of faith and *not* believe in God? Well, a successful marriage requires that both spouses have complete faith in each other, which has nothing to do with whether they attend the same church or believe in the same God concept. Sending your 15 year old daughter out on her first date takes a great deal of faith (a prayer wouldn't hurt either). But faith in this regard always focuses on people and on a certain kind of expectation from those people. And developing this kind of faith involves observing the behavior of someone (or some process) over a period of time long enough to see a pattern. It's this demonstrated pattern you believe in.

Let's look at two examples of the latter: The first is Old Faithful in Yellowstone National Park. (Honestly, no pun intended.) The famous geyser erupts every hour—no matter what the weather is or if the tour bus has a flat? Then there's the situation where, lacking any evidence regarding previous behavior, you still want to have faith. A new hairdresser, a car repair shop you haven't used before, a new lawn service that tells you not to worry, grubs are their middle name...and so on. The auto repairman in question delivers on his promises, and you're delighted and amazed. You're a...*believer!* This grows over time until the guy sells the shop to his cousin. Then you have to go back to square one. But you see where we're going...it takes repetitive trials to develop faith in future performance, whether it's a mechanic or a marriage partner. (There may be a joke in there somewhere, but I'm not going to touch it.)

People who are fervent believers have expectations about God's interventions, but having these met 100% of the time is not only unrealistic, it's not what God is about. He is not Daddy Warbucks or the Fairy Godmother who, with one touch of the wand, will give us everything we ask for. There are those televangelists who preach the "health and wealth" schtick, assuring their viewers that God wants them to be successful. The last time I checked, God calls us to be loving, patient and kind, but not successful, despite the Prayer of Jabez crowd.

Faith in God

The power of doctrine and tradition

Perhaps the most poignant example that comes to mind concerns the Holocaust. Knowing with certain dread that the gas chambers lay only a hundred yards away, millions of Jews kept praying to their God even after the steel doors clanged shut behind them. This kind of relationship with their God was thousands of years old—it was as though it was organic...primal like their DNA helix.

All but a few of them retained their faith, even though all who entered the chambers perished. The few who abandoned God did so because they found it hard to believe a God that would have allowed the horrors they had suffered up until that point, would step in now. And did he? To gain insight into this agonizing question, you need to talk to a survivor of the camps, one of those very old people who still has the number tattooed on the inside arm just below the elbow. The numbers do not fade over time, and from what I have observed, neither do the memories. So how strong can a religion based on faith be?

A group of Jews in a concentration camp decided that enough was enough, and that God should be on trial for allowing them to suffer so. Witnesses were called, a jury impaneled, and after hours of testimony, the jury reached their verdict. Guilty! After the judge read it aloud, he said, "All right, now let's light the candles. It's the start of the Sabbath."

Even though they had levied a judgment, they could not let go of their core beliefs. The prisoners were able to summon strength from a source whose religious roots go so deep they cannot be pulled out of the ground. Yes, we found God guilty, they were saying but we cannot walk away from him. If we do, we lose our identity, our reason for being. It took England's Lloyd George to capture the strength of this faith in words that though written 15 years before the Holocaust, serve as a timeless epitaph.

You may say you have been oppressed
And persecuted—that has been your power!
You have been hammered into very fine steel,
And that is why you have never been broken.

Belief in a non-spiritual God

Is faith required or not?

I'll answer my own question. Yes, it's required, but it's a different kind of faith. In an earlier discussion of a collective conscience God, we pondered the issue of whether anyone hears your prayer. Since you're not praying to a spiritual God, then (1) how do you communicate with your target group and (2) how do you know that it's working? First, since you've observed their past behavior, you must have some faith in their future responses. Second (remember my analogy of the married couple?) it's quite possible to communicate effectively without words. And a lot of scientific evidence exists to prove people can send thought waves through the air—ESP. And finally, if your faith is strong enough, you just believe. Ever heard that? Still not convinced it works? Maybe you don't have enough faith in...other people's faith.

In discussions with others about the faith of those who believe in one of the collective conscience God concepts, invariably I hear the following: "But if they really believed in God the way I do, they would know that God hears them and will respond." I'd give that a A+ for faith but a D- for tolerance and understanding. We've said this several times, but once more won't hurt: faith is like Joseph's coat of many colors. It's good and no doubt useful to have absolute faith that your spiritual God hears and responds to you, but it's intolerant to question or denigrate another kind of faith that someone believes works just as well as yours does. Having faith in a spiritual God can make you a better person if you adopt your God's spirituality.

Something else—in my conversations, I've heard from people who tell me that the act of dialogue with God—whether one calls it prayer or meditation—can create an intimacy that in turn generates a feeling of peace and contentment. A healing of a troubled spirit. Calms the storms that may beset us. Scripture is replete with examples of this. One friend tells me her favorite is from Psalm 46: "be still...and know that I am God."

Faith and miracles

"Honest to God, it happened"

This is a touchy subject. Very touchy. In fact, for some, it's the great divide that separates real faith from make believe, real believers from pretenders. For others, this is a minor mile marker on the freeway of moral behavior. And then, there are people who don't believe that any of the biblical miracles really happened. Still others are conflicted over which miracles to believe and which to reject—further, whether believing all of the miracles happened is a requirement for believing in God. To thicken the broth, people's views on miracles have changed over time, just like their views on everything else—sex, dress, politics and yes, religion. The fact is: events and things the possibility of which the "experts" would have deemed miraculous at the time, have a habit of morphing into the commonplace.

"I think there is a world market for five...maybe six computers."
Thomas Watson, Chairman and Founder of IBM, 1943

"I have traveled the length and breadth of this country, talking with the best people, and I can assure you that data processing is a fad that won't last out the year."
Ralph Franklin, Editor-in-Chief, the business books division of Prentice Hall Publishers, 1957

"The wireless music box—some people call it the radio—has no imaginable commercial value. Who would
pay for a message sent to people you can't even see?"
Bankers urging David Sarnoff not to invest in the radio

"The abdomen, the chest and the brain will forever be
closed off to the surgeon's scalpel."
Sir John Ericksen, Chief surgeon to Queen Victoria, 1873

"I have never heard of anything more absurd than ac-
quiring New Mexico and California. They are not worth
one dollar.
Daniel Webster, 1848

"There is no possible combination of machinery that
can move a flying machine through the air."
Simon Newton, 1903

"The population of the earth decreases every day. In
another 100 years, the earth will be nothing but a
desert."
Montesquieu, 1743

"The atomic bomb is the biggest fool thing we have ever
done. It will never go off, and I speak as an expert in
explosives."
Admiral William Leahy, 1945

"Frankly, we don't like their sound, and anyway, gui-
tar music is on the way out."
Decca Recording Co. rejecting the Beatles, 1962

If you find these hilarious, you're not alone. Getting serious—with regard to the biblical miracles as reported, people' s
attitudes range from "hard core literalists" to...well, incurable
skeptics. Each side thinks the other's bread is not quite done.
As I said in the beginning, it's a touchy subject! But we have to
deal with it, and now is better than later.

What were some of the miracles?

Miracles in just about every faith

Probably the best known Christian miracle is that Jesus is God's son, resulting from a virgin birth. I don't mean to imply these are the most important miracles: (consider that John Wesley preached more than 50,000 sermons in his lifetime, and not one on the virgin birth. Moreover, the first, and regarded as the most reliable gospel writer, Mark, devoted not one word to the nativity). Certainly, these events form the bedrock of traditional Christian faith. And there are others associated with Jesus: calling forth Lazarus, walking on water and feeding the multitudes with a few fishes and loaves. Of course, Jews have their miracles, too. The parting of the Red Sea (actually, it was the Sea of Reeds—blame a nearsighted copyist) and the temple lamp that burned 8 days on only 1 day's worth of oil—the Hanukkah miracle. (If we could repeat that, BP, Exxon and others of that ilk would have what my mother used to call a "conniption fit.")

It should be noted that neither Judaism nor Christianity has cornered the miracles market. Mohammed, an illiterate, while being crushed in God's arms, began reciting the holy scripture that would become the Koran. And let us not forget Joseph Smith, the founder of Mormonism, who dug up some gold tablets near Palmyra, N.Y. on which was engraved the entire Book of Mormon. (It should be noted that no one but Mr. Smith ever saw the tablets.) Last but hardly least, God has his miracles, too. He created the world in just 6 days, although linguistic scholars agree that in the original Hebrew, the word for day, "yom," chronologically could have meant almost anything. Our point is that over the long span of recorded history, the reported list of miracles would fill many books, but remember—I like trees.

Did the miracles really happen like they were written?

Is that the most important question?

It all depends on whom you ask and what you read. O.K. then, but who's right? You already know the answer to this, too. It all depends on what you believe. And how do you learn what to believe? A definite no brainer: when you're young, you listen to what your parents believe. Then as you grow older, you listen to people who either believe in miracles or don't—these include well meaning relatives, authors, religious leaders, the requisite number of drunks in bars and the like. So...where did all these people learn whether miracles actually happened or not? It all depends on...(is there an echo in here?)

Whether the miracles really happened is not the point at all! As far as I'm concerned, the only relevant point is whether you believe they did. If you believe—fine! But that alone does not and will not make you either a good person or more religious—oops, change that to spiritual. It simply means you believe in the biblical miracles. If you don't believe, that's fine too, and it doesn't make you any less moral or a bad person. It just means you may get into arguments in church if you don't keep quiet. But there's a wrinkle: some people tell me their religious leader says they *have* to believe all of the miracles happened, just like it's written because...wait a minute, I have to stop and pull over:

> **It's that word "written." The Bible has been through more versions, editions, translations and revisions (think of the word "spin,") than any book ever printed. Popes, kings, rabbis, preachers, scholars, printers, publishers, church leaders, plus various and sundry wonks have all had their way with it. Stuff has been taken out, stories omitted—what about the "Lost Gospels?" And the Dead Sea Scrolls that caused a theological "faith quake." So when someone says, "the Bible says," which Bible are they talking about? Did you know that Ptolemy of**

Egypt appointed 70 scholars to translate the Bible from Hebrew into Greek? That ought to be your first clue— I mean, did you ever know 70 academics to agree on anything? But lest you think I'm playing fast and loose, I'll defer to the last gospel writer, John, who has this to say at the very end of his narrative: "And I suppose that if all the other events in Jesus' life were written, the whole world could hardly contain the books." So if some things were admittedly left out, then might not others have been put in? The classic literary techniques of reduction and redaction. Think about it!

Conclusion? Knowing who actually said what, about what and to whom is tough enough; and interpreting the miracles is hardly simple. Now throw in the *religious* factor, and the equation tilts—it's all muddied up. Are you being sanctioned and potentially distanced from your spiritual God—not because you are a bad person, but simply because you are a *questioning* person or a *searching* person? Are we supposed to suck up scripture through a straw or can we use our brains and try to figure out what the writers might have meant? As Galileo said, "I do not feel obligated to believe that the same God who has endowed us with sense, reason and intellect has intended us to forgo their use." You see, when people tried to question things like this hundreds of years ago, they were burned at the stake. (Over time, that punishment was replaced by something called committees.)

Do miracles continue to happen? Millions of people believe they do...on a storm swept sea on March 21, 1748, the slave ship, *The Greyhound,* was taking on water. A sailor, John Newton, too exhausted to pump was tied to the helm to keep the ship into the wind. Newton prayed for deliverance, knowing all on board were doomed. "Miraculously" (as some said later) the ship did not go down, and eventually, Newton became a minister. Years later, he wrote in his diary, "only God's amazing grace could and did take a rude, profane, slave-trading sailor and turn him into a child of God." John Newton died at the age of 82, and among the gifts he left the world is "Amazing Grace," the most frequently sung hymn of all time. Do miracles still happen today? If you have the insight to recognize them, they do.

Well, if these events weren't miracles, what were they?

A look at the options

First up, the parting of the Red Sea (Sea of Reeds). The most common alternative explanation of this is an extremely low tide on a tidal bar, occurring simultaneously with a strong favorable wind that taken together, rolled back the sea long enough for the Israelites to escape. I see folks at the beach every summer walking on an offshore bar when the wind and tide are right. If that were the case, then why was it written the way it was? One answer is that myth is one of the most powerful literary devices known. It can make a character "larger than life." Look at Jack and the Beanstalk; actually, forget Jack and concentrate on the beanstalk that "grew to the sky." Look at Paul Bunyan and his ox, Babe. As the Greek poet, Homer, illustrated in the Iliad and the Odyssey, myth has the power to capture the human imagination like the wind picking up a leaf. Through the wonder and magic of words, we are sent soaring into a realm of what if and wow! The biblical writers certainly had powerful imaginations, along with being first rate wordsmiths—combine that with a strong faith and...well, the sky's the limit.

Myths are also used as metaphors. When we read that Jesus "walked on the water," the idea behind this was to calm the fears of those in the boat who were doubting and anxious. The message? With faith—however you view it and whatever its source—you can calm the storms in your life. We all have them at one time or another, and if we're not careful, we may drown in a sea of depression, rage, self pity or all the above. What better metaphor than a storm on the Sea of Galilee, which for the record is subject to sudden, violent squalls. The writer knew that and used it. Good man.

Now the miracle of the virgin birth. That kind of story did not begin with Jesus. Attis, Son of God of Phrygia, was born to a virgin mother called "savior." Krishna, Son of God of India, was born to a virgin mother centuries before Jesus; some say he was crucified to a tree and rose from the dead. Dionysus or Bacchus, Son of God of Greece, was born to a virgin mother, turned water into wine, was crucified and rose from the dead. There are a dozen more historical instances of virgin birth from nations around the world. So what could the historical writers have been trying to describe? Let's examine the facts—objectively and dispassionately. We know that Jesus' virgin birth was not part of the early Christian doctrine or tradition. It is not to be found in the teaching of the apostles. The virgin birth is thought by many scholars to be a product of the large pagan conversions to Christianity that occurred in the late 2nd century. Church leaders knew this would resonate strongly with the pagan mind-set and the legends that were part of their culture. Also,

> **In the original Greek texts, the words used to describe Mary's condition are as follows: "a maiden shall conceive." The Greek word used is *parthenos* which does not mean virgin. Later, when Matthew was translated into Latin, the words became "a virgin shall conceive." Again, let's zoom in on the text. In the Hebrew, the word was *almah*. It's right there in Isaiah's prophecy, and *almah* means maiden not virgin. Neither parthenos nor *almah* refers to a biological virgin.**

And what of Jesus being the physical son of God? First of all, since God is not a human—a fact most accept—then there is no sperm or ova or DNA or anything remotely resembling that. Remember: it was Gabriel who brought the news to Mary (real name, Miriam) that the conception within her "was or-

dained by heaven." Gabriel didn't say anything about God being the paternal, biological or natural father, only the *spiritual* father. Joseph and Mary pondered how the offspring of humans could be a child of divine destiny and finally concluded, they had been chosen to become the parents of the *Moschiach*...the Messiah.

At that time nothing was known, thought or said about God actually fathering the child: that idea appeared in the gospels some seventy years later. But even then, why refer to Jesus as the Son of God? Why not? What greater adoration could you bestow on a child than to call it, son of God? Wasn't this an absolutely stunning and brilliant way to give even more spiritual meaning to what Jesus had said and done during his life? Moreover, seventy years later, who was to say it wasn't so? Thus, a Godly blessing such as this may have been turned into one of the most compelling and enduring myths of Christianity.

Next question: does every Christian believe these stories literally? In surveys like those in chapter 6, one out of three does not. More to the point, many respected biblical scholars do not even believe that the credibility of Christianity is affected by the virgin birth or the paternity of Jesus. They are willing to accept them (and other miracles) for what they were: myths, stories, affectionate tales, prophesy remembered and examples of adoration—in short, the stuff that is the heart and soul of spirituality. The fact is: if Christian can be defined as one who follows the moral teachings and precepts of Jesus—who left his followers with a two word imperative—follow me!—then the conscious and spiritual act of obedience in following him is not dependent on your accepting the virgin birth or the fact that he was "God's son." Indeed, Jesus himself never said or claimed to be "the son of God." Rather he said, "who do *they* say that I am?" And if you think I'm picking on Christians—whoa! Back up. I could just as easily have said to a Jewish reader, "your standing as a Jew in no way depends on what you believe about the Hanukkah oil or the Sea of Reeds...and to a Muslim, your acceptance by Allah does not hinge on whether you believe that

Mohammed, a confirmed illiterate, began reciting the holy scripture while crushed in God's arms. Back to the start—the virgin birth was probably meant to elevate him and set Jesus apart from other self-proclaimed messiahs of the period. The parting of the waters was a symbol of God's power as he rescued his people. And God giving Mohammed the Koran but taking 23 years to do it may be a metaphor for both the difficulty of learning and the value of the end result.

Faith and miracles

Summing it all up

Here's where I am on this: miracles may have been real, they may be myth, they may be history enlarged, they may be history forgotten, they may be history invented, they may be methods of adoration and respect, or they may be potent combinations of all of these. In fact, after thousands of years, no one really knows for sure, including the person who leads your congregation. But what we *do* know is that miracles and myths are part of religion's beautiful and enduring tapestry. Events and behavior that people regarded as extraordinary, all embroidered into the fabric of history.

- Accepting miracles literally does not in itself make you more religious, more pious or more moral.

- If you want to exemplify those traits, you have to embrace them through your behavior in the here and now.

- And the converse is equally true: not believing these does not make you a lesser person or a second class member of your faith. It just means your primary focus is on what you are doing to live out the golden rule rather than on endless debates and disputes about what happened (or didn't happen) thousands of years ago. Don't let anybody tell you otherwise.

Wrap? Consider again these two words: *orthodoxy* (correct or right thinking) and *orthopraxy*—right living. It is the difference between, on the one hand, this formalized, sometimes creaking, construct called religion and on the other, a dynamic model of compassionate moral behavior. And whoever said that what was orthodox was right anyhow?

Okay, let's get it out on the table:

Is there anything bad about faith?

That's what my mother would have called an *awful* question. I can hear her now when I was ten years old. *Dick, you shouldn't talk about things like that.* Why, Mom? *Because it's not nice and you just shouldn't. Now forget it.* Mom was a very literate woman, one of the first female insurance underwriters in Philadelphia history, an awesome banjo player, an Eastern Star Worthy Matron and a Red Cross instructor during WWII.

As I started writing this section, I was wondering. Can we ever have too much faith? Is that like having too much money, or too much influence or too much good looks? Mmm...I don't think so. First, let's be sure we are talking about the same definition of faith (after all we've given you a generous handful). The faith we're discussing now is faith in your God whatever that may be. Does that clear up your confusion? No...? Well, let me restate the question. Can you foresee a situation where having too much faith in your God could affect your ability to persevere?

My sense is that most people who believe in God see those decisions we call "life altering' as a joint effort between themselves and their God—a combination of work and faith if you will. Of course, in a sense, *all* decisions are joint, which takes us back to what I told you in an earlier chapter: "Pray as if everything depended on God; work as if everything depended on you."

That's about as good a description as I can come up with of the "divine partnership." But now a caveat—just because you think your God hasn't done his or her part doesn't mean you can kick back or slack off from time to time. And if for some reason you fail to hold up your end of the bargain—and things still go well—who or what is to say you won't exploit this and slack off even more? Too far fetched for you? Let's rewind to *Elmer Gantry* again. As Preacher Gantry's professed faith increased, his morality tanked. But that's only a movie. True, but then there's Jim Bakker and Jimmy Swaggart and Father Coughlin (the sick, anti-Semitic priest of the '30's). And Osama bin Laden and Rabbi Kahane. (For those of you who aren't familiar with the last name, this guy was...well, rabid. Let's leave it there.) The point is, all of these men professed faith, but they were all moral miscreants. And the second point is that no matter how much faith you say you have, God as your partner might help you lift up the rear of the wagon but he can't pick up your "moral axle." Viewed as a contractor, God says , "if you will do this, I will do that." And when I say *this,* that includes morality. Your ethical core. Whatever goodness resides within you and is made manifest by your behavior. And you simply cannot substitute more faith for less morality. That stuff is too precious to be sold by the pound or the yard. The two are just not substitutable.

Can faith dampen rational thinking and critical examination?

Another question Mom might call "awful."

I'm sorry, Mom, but I have to deal with this, and the answer is yes—if you let it. Having faith in a God is "good," but I have the feeling that God doesn't want you to dump the important decisions in his lap. That's not the way the historical contract reads. Besides, you're the one on the scene, staring the problem right in the face. So it's really your call, isn't it? The way it was supposed to turn out was that God gave us spirituality so we might grow both up and out—like say, a tree. Being in balance with all around us. We're factory equipped to make good choices. Sensible. Life supporting. Love enhancing. And demurring to God when we go weak in the knees is not the same as asking God's guidance (and blessing) on what we are about to undertake. I don't think that's the way to build either self confidence or sharpen our decision-making skills, and I think if the Bible tells us anything, it tells us that. Chapter and verse.

Why do people do it then? Why do they throw up their hands and give you that old saw, "oh, God will take care of it." (Translated: I just discovered a streak of physical or moral cowardice or laziness or pride (fill in the blank) and I can't afford for the news to get around.) Folks, by a certain age we learned the basic rules: our job was to educate and train ourselves to deal with problems and practice what we'd learned in order to deal with a life of decision-making. And if you *haven't* done that—meaning you sneaked under the tent without paying— you might not get to enjoy the show...and it's the greatest show on earth!

And if you think you can renege on your part of the contract, I think you're whistling in the dark. You may bob and weave, skip and scam, slip over and under, but you want to know something? I suspect that God is neither fooled nor amused. After all, that's why he's God. Right? And you can jump up and down in your favorite house of worship, put some money in the plate, memorize the verses and sing all the choruses, but it's like Bishop James Thomas (the first African American bishop in the United Methodist Church) once said: "all that jumping up in the air is fine, but what are you going to do for God once you're back on the ground?"

And what about those who don't believe?

We just can't walk off and leave atheists and agnostics standing here all alone in our narrative. It's not right. It's not moral. It's not forgiving. It's not loving. It's not, well...God-like. What gives you, me, any of us, the right to point fingers at these people and pass judgment and sling a sentence such as "you're going to hell." Only God has the answer to that, and he's not talking.

Or at least, he's not a finger pointer. That much we do know, and I offer that as perhaps the best Bible lesson of all time— *judge not....* I'm wondering...do people who believe in a non-spiritual God have this same problem, that is, lack of self-confidence? Do they delegate decisions "upward," and cop a plea when it comes to making the tough calls? There is no evidence that I know of to show that, on the one hand, lack of self-confidence, or on the other, the ability to make rational decisions is the sole province of those who believe in a spiritual God. We said it earlier: collective conscience folks have faith. They pray. They have reasonable expectations that they are heard, and they also have expectations about some kind of response.

It's my guess—I hope, an informed one—that about the same proportion of them might come up a little short on what we've been calling "this." Our end of the bargain. Our part of the deal. Our earnest money. Our bred-in-the-bone promise: Yes, God, we're going to stand in the docket and the breach. And we might not achieve perfect attendance at religious services (in fact, we might not show up at all) but then, you never really cared about that in the first place, did you?

CHAPTER 8

GOD, RELIGION AND HUMAN BEHAVIOR

Is God a behaviorist?

W ell, if you mean, is he board certified, has a license and all that, I don't know—and I'm not about to ask. But in a way, that's begging the question. So let's start by defining our terms. A behavioral scientist is someone who uses anthropology, psychology and sociology (along with logic and common sense) to develop normative rules in order to improve the way people—well, behave. That covers everything from two-year-olds throwing tantrums and flicking their spoonful of crunchy critters on the ceiling to grown-ups who turn into dictators and other exemplars of *homo sapiens.*

- Anthropology: Looks at the different kinds of people on earth: their appearance, social and cultural customs and relationships.

- Psychology: Deals with the mind and how its emotional machinery changes gears.

- Sociology: Deals with social relationships as part of organization and change.

Those are our working tools, and I'd have to say the three taken together make up a pretty good description of God's focus. Not to take away from God, but all successful leaders, in any area of human endeavor, sooner or later master the principles of behavioral science. Now, a lot of people believe these skills come naturally to us, and sadly, this is one of the great misconceptions of the last 5000 years. Some, even if given two lifetimes, would never master these; others pick it up with ease like fielding a slow grounder to third. Back to the question, then: is God a behavioral scientist? *What if I say, no, Dick?* Hey, what did I tell you in Chapter One. Reading this book is purely voluntary. I am not out to bash "clubs," and there is no quiz at the end. Accordingly, you can fast forward or rewind at any time. Be my guest. And thank you for having stayed with me thus far.

But back to our question—is God that practitioner? Let's test our definition: God sees all the people of our planet, takes note of their differences and observes where and how they live; how they relate to each other, how they're organized, deals with their thoughts and feelings and presides over all the changes that have occurred since the first tick of the clock. O.K., my vote is that among the other hats God wears, he *is* a behaviorist, and enough of one to put most of us engineers to shame.

In the first paragraph of this chapter, we mentioned "normative rules" with an end toward improving human behavior. If normative means "right," or "the way things ought to be" (such as your teens ought to be keeping their rooms cleaned up) then normative is a goal we reach for, but unfortunately may never attain. This is a good place to pause and visualize the Ten Commandments, one of God's earliest gifts to humanity. They are certainly normative. Great packaging, too. Conclusion? God has a normative plan for all of us—and as we've stated, has the requisite credentials to help us toward that goal. Notice I didn't say *take* us. Do you remember in the 4th chapter when I said it was O.K. to help your kids with their homework, but not wise to *do* it for them? It applies here as well. Exactly how, then, does God motivate us toward an acceptable set of behaviors? That may be the most important result of spirituality, yet another one of God's mysterious gifts.

But what about people who *don't* believe in a spiritual God? Do they get a ticket to ride on the normative train? After all, just because you believe that God exists as the conscience of a lot of people—as opposed to a spirit or an anthropomorphic being—this doesn't disqualify you. We can assume that if your reference group (in the current lingo, those you hang with) is fairly large, and allowed to think freely and independently) the force of their current and flow would eventually move you toward normative. Besides, we can't discount the value and effect of plain old common sense. Put another way, having a Ph.D. in psychology doesn't guarantee that your interpersonal behavior hits the top of the charts. To the contrary, some world class nut cases are found on college faculties!

A word about this word "religious."

Exactly what are we talking about here?

Let's start with *adherence* to a religion, which means belonging to a group of like-minded believers. You attend, pay, participate and contribute in other ways, but that's all quantitative. On the qualitative side, there are meanings such as conscientious, compassionate, devout, godly and moral—now we're talking about behavior. And given the time, energy and resources that humans invest in religion, we would hope to find a strong correlation between membership and moral behavior. Although many believe such a correlation exists—and casual observation suggests this is the case—it's never been proven or disproved So if it hasn't been proven, why do people stick with it? (We covered this in Chapter 5, *Why Do People Need God?)* But wait—can't you know and enjoy God and behave morally without being affiliated with a religious organization? Sure. We addressed this in Chapter 7, *Faith in God and Faith in Yourself*

Which brings us to an early conclusion: telling people you are religious—and going a step further, demonstrating it by perfect attendance at religious services—does not win you the Good Housekeeping seal of approval (on earth or anywhere else). However, it may evoke from others a positive *perception* of your morality. Thus, if you are a sometimes participant or never come at all, it's not uncommon for those that fill the pews on a regular basis to draw some inferences: to whit, if you are conspicuous by your absence, their reasoning goes, how can you be religious and therefore, how can your behavior be moral?

So is the converse true? If they see you there every week, how does this color their perception? C'mon, now! You know very well that regular attendance is often equated with moral behavior. But the fact is: moral people have never had an exclusive franchise on brains. Evil people are intelligent, too—sometimes genius level—and they often use this intelligence to devise fascinating con games. The business headlines of the past couple of years in particular should leave no doubt about this. Some of the most immoral people I have ever known attend religious services regularly, often compulsively. (Do you know some people like this too?) And as a corollary of that, could the worst apples in this barrel have concluded that compulsive religious attendance is one of the best trade-offs they can make? After all, compared to *being* moral, plunking your body in the pews is a fairly simple thing to do (relatively painless except for an occasional boring sermon) and may cause others to see an imaginary halo around your head. Don't tell me that some of the worst miscreants in the Enron debacle, and others too numerous to mention, didn't show their smiling faces in some religious body when their Gulfstream V wasn't available. And if you are successful in winning social approval, even while your hand is picking other pockets, it could become a habit. Indeed, is it possible that these people leave services feeling...well, *forgiven* for some or all of their bad deeds? On the other hand, I believe that God does have great patience. Uh oh, that sounds like the start of a sermon, and that doesn't fall within my job description.

> **A well known practical theologian and guest professor at one seminary made the observation that people constantly complained to him, "there's an awful lot of sin in organized religion." His answer was: yes, and there's an awful lot of sin in the *world;* "what is a house of worship," he continued, "but a slice of the world outside." Putting "God in a box" as the saying goes, is no guarantee of anything, other than proof of the persuasive abilities of those who head up the building fund. Church (substitute any word you like that identifies the building on the corner) is not something you "go to." It identifies something you *are!* This is also the same man who told his students, "in every congregation you will find one or two people divinely inspired to drive you crazy." Just change congregation to classroom, and I know whereof he speaks.**

All right, let's focus on two different groups. The first is the segment we just referenced: immoral individuals who attend services, uh, religiously and wear that as a badge of good behavior. Do these people believe in God? My strong sense is that if you asked them, the answer would be a unanimous "yes." Of course, you'd get the same response if you asked them if they believed in the law of gravity. The only difference is they wouldn't be jumping up and down about it. But let's dig down to the core of this issue, which is, not whether they believe in God, but rather do they know what commitment is required of them *as a result of this belief?* And secondly, do you think this kind of behavior merits God's blessing. In some cases, that's when that shiny, glazed look comes over their faces, they draw themselves up to their full height and start to tell you how much money they've given during the past year, how many committees they've served on...*ad infinitum ad nauseam.*

Am I alarmed by any of this? No, and I don't believe that God is surprised, though I would guess a bit saddened. You see, I believe that over time, the basically moral world that we inhabit can deal with these pretenders. Some will continue to show up dressed to the nines on a consistent basis and play the game as long as they can. Others will be rooted out or exposed by the light of spirituality— a ray of sunshine bright enough to stream through even the dingiest basement window.

So much for group one. Now what about the others, whom we'll call religious zealots, and I mean that in the most pejorative sense of the word, i.e., fanatics who perpetrate evil in God's name. We've already given these the once over earlier in the book so all they get here is a sideswipe.

- The Crusaders believed God was firmly on their side and that he sanctioned their murderous behavior.

- Pope Innocent VIII viewed his own brand of witchcraft and terror as being the will of God.

- The Muslim conquerors of Spain felt Allah had strongly endorsed their 15th century reign of tyranny and slaughter.

- Europeans invoked God's blessing on their relentless persecutions of the Jews for several centuries, and Hitler's "final solution" for the Jews was planned and carried out under the eyes of the Catholic Church, not only in Germany and Poland but in Rome as well.

I think we can safely assume that God did not sanction any of this behavior but was a saddened and angry observer. The question to ask of Yahweh is, why not send a flood or monster earthquake or fire from the heavens? Why didn't God intervene? Why indeed? Theologians and religious leaders have sermonized, agonized and debated over this for what seems like forever. As we know, the spiritual God most folks believe in did none of these. At least, not in observable form. What he *did* do was provide his believers with succor, spirituality and faith even as they perished. Now briefly switch your mental gears from a spirit God to a more secular God concept. If God is the part of us we call *conscience,* then all this fits. We do bad things, thus if God is us, God is part of our immorality and does immoral things too. If this bothers you, remember that the Old Testament God was murderous, brutal and inconsistent: one time, he instructed the Hebrews to go into a village and kill every man, woman and child and leave no one alive except the virgins. So? Why can't a secular God be part of immoral behavior at times?

Nonbelievers who behave morally

Can an atheist or agnostic be moral?

Of course, and it's not an oxymoron. These individuals are fierce in their contention that rectitude is not a product of a spiritual God, a secular God or any God, for that matter, and can be learned and put into practice independent of any of these God concepts. It poses an intriguing theological question, the resolution of which presents itself in their revealed behavior and in centuries of endless debate.

I have a very dear friend, an atheist (I have others as well) who is more moral in her day-to-day behavior than just about anyone I know personally. A true Golden Ruler. You could use every adjective in the Girl Scout oath to describe her and still fall short. When I ask her where she learned morality, she tells me "from reading books" (she is not a Bible reader, at least not in her adult life) "and from observing others." When I ask her the source of her moral strength and conviction for her unflagging application of the Golden Rule, she doesn't answer "God's spirituality" but instead credits it to her internal conviction that she owes this to society in exchange for her life.

Wow! If that doesn't ignite a spark of humility and awe within you, I don't know what will. Many people believe you can be religious—that is, exhibiting true moral behavior—without believing in God. Surveys say the majority of people don't believe that, but never mind that—it's what *you* believe that counts. You can be a believer without being a "belonger." You may eschew doctrine but be divinely guided in your life application. You may never darken the doors of a religious institution but knock on the doors of the hurting and needy. Of course, the implications of this for the numbers-driven monolith of organized religion have terrifying implications for the bean counters. What if you gave a service and nobody came? The more people who find and practice their morality outside the doors of that building on the corner...well, its bottom line may take a dip and dive.

Question: does God smile upon these "outsiders," the moral atheists and agnostics? Does God love them? Or does God reject their efforts out of hand? I suggest the answer depends on whose God we are talking about—as well as whose intermediary is interpreting God's answer for you. Consider: if your God has established normative behavioral objectives for humans, and he created people with that goal in mind, then if they so behave, why *wouldn't* he love them? I mean, doesn't God want God-like behavior from us? Does it make sense for us to measure goodness and kindness by the hollow standard of attendance at religious services? The formal exercise of responsive reading? The repetitive reading of liturgy? Must we earn a gold star and have our name inscribed on a plaque in the narthex (that means *foyer* to us but it's Greek for *casket)* before we can qualify as moral? God-like? God-loving. God-loved? Think about it!

Dick, you're asking too much of me.

I know. Isn't that the whole idea?

But you're asking me to reject an idea that's almost like a second skin: namely, that morality requires belief in God. You're asking me to consider whether humans can be moral without such a belief. Which is tantamount to rejecting the God I've always believed in for something...something I don't even understand. Wrong! I'm not asking you to do anything of the kind. I'm asking you to think logically and clearly and honestly about human behavior. *Believe* what you want to *believe.* That's fine with me as long as you've given it a proper hearing with your head and heart and are comfortable with your conclusion. Just make sure you cut everyone else the same deal. Tragically, many religious leaders reject this model of "live and let live," as though they have the one, true and only God. My way or the highway. You either believe what they believe or they damn you to hell for eternity.

Dr. Albert Schweitzer (we've cited him before) believed that too many people spend their religious lives on their knees trying to barter a ticket to eternal bliss rather than on their feet, dispensing kindness and healing to those unfortunates who are hurting. He saw this as the great folly of institutional (dogmatic) religion. Ultimately, he had little time for theological brain draining but found all the time in the world for the sick and needy.

So which religion is right? Or is any of them? *How do you know?* What channeler or middle man has the answer? *How do you know?* Which words of the 775,693 in the Bible are the most important? *How do you know?* Should you go charismatic? Evangelical? Formalist? Fundamentalist? Prophetic? Orthodox? Reform? Millennial? *How do you know?* Solemn? Sedate? Sensational? Revelational? Revolutionary? *How do you know?*

Now are you starting to see the dimensions of this dilemma? Its boundaries reach farther than our minds can fathom. But that's why God gave us imaginations and the gift of judgment. And at this point, if you're feeling a bit lost and can't pick the "right one," that's all right. Because that's not what it's about. *All* of them could be right. The real question is: which one is right for *you?* Which one quickens your heart? Which belief system fits you like your favorite walking shoes or a cherished sweater? After all, the Golden Rule is not about what we read or listen to or stand up and recite or study with our brain on fixed focus. It's about what we do.

Religion and moral behavior

They used to go together like lox and bagels.

But perhaps no more! Does that rock you? Does it step on your toes, like a good preacher is supposed to do? I think that's what it will take to get both our minds in gear, so step out of the box, please—here comes a wild pitch.

Is it possible that religion and morality were never linked to *start with?* That they have not been best buds or bedfellows for centuries? If you'll recall, we began Chapter 2, A brief history of God, with the idea that the ancients experienced thunder, lightning, floods and the occasional eclipse and as a result, began a program of ceremonial offerings in order to appease whatever was up there, make it go away. You know—get back to quiet. We've got to "make nice," said the medicine man, and make nice they did, not the least of which was human sacrifices. Whatever it took to made the rivers recede, the locusts bug out, the sun reappear and the monsoons stop. And most important, to raise crop yields (the USDA probably hasn't done that well since) not to mention raise sexual performance. I haven't seen any numbers on this, but I have the hunch that lots of men may have stopped praying for help after Viagra came on the scene.

All that sounds reasonable enough to us now. More and more people started believing that God and morality were linked. So what happened to sever that bond? Well, for starters, over time people observed that as religion grew quantitatively, evil did not abate. What was a poor tribe to do? Folks pondered this as they grew increasingly fed up with the immoral behavior of many of their religious leaders and came to the inevitable but sad conclusion that maybe religious practice and morality were often *not* linked. It is, after all, a fact that more people have been killed in wars fought for religious reasons than for any other. That's not exactly a sterling testimony to the efficacy of man's absurd religious theatre. In the case of Pope Innocent VIII and others of his ilk, of any stripe, "absurd" could be changed to "abominable." (More about the machinations and merchandising coming up in the next chapter.)

We've already catalogued the evils and abominations of religious systems a few pages back, and we won't repeat them—other than to say that today, even though religion is alive, there is no let up in crime, pornography, child abuse, regional wars,

AIDS, hatred, terrorism and selfish commercialism. Intelligent people can connect the dots.

Talking the talk or walking the walk. Speaking the word or living the Word. That's what it's about. Gold stars and pretty certificates are given out for those who show up every time the doors are opened but for whom moral goodness is often eclipsed by what Jesus (and many others) called the worst sin of all—religious pride. It's that frame of mind that leads some to say, "you're going to hell, and I'm glad of it." On the other side of the coin, sometimes those who live the word, often with great risk, get zapped!

> **Case in point: In Durham, North Carolina, recently, the assistant manager of a convenience store observed a wanted criminal enter the premises and quickly reported it to the police. The gendarmes showed up and arrested the culprit. On hearing about this diligence and heroic act, the home office of the chain promptly fired the employee, claiming that she had "endangered her coworkers." (Where is my Mylanta when I need it?) What we have here is a clear case of "no good deed goes unpunished." A moral and courageous act results in loss of livelihood. No gold star. Just a fast pass to the unemployment line. Funny thing: the president of the chain thought no one would notice what he had done, but when the press gave the story life, he began back peddling and lying and finally rehired her.**

Talking the talk or walking the walk. Remember how much money is spent annually paying religious leaders and how many dollars have gone into religious bricks and mortar to say nothing of books and movies. Walking the walk is not the great institution that the "talking" is.

- Whistle-blowers lose their jobs and if not, are shunned.

- Environmental polluters get token fines.

- Kids who cheat in school get real-time forgiveness because punishment may damage their self-esteem.

- Teachers who flunk non-performers get sanctioned by principals.

- Wall Street crooks who cost others their life savings get wrist-slap fines and suspended sentences.

- And politicians have given pork a perennial bad name.

It's a bit like rats and cheese: if you double up on the cheese and disable the traps, you get an entirely different kind of rat behavior. Harvard's B. F. Skinner, the granddaddy of all behaviorists, pioneered these early experiments and found it was true with pigeons, too. Naturally, your author had to do his own casual empiricism. I discovered that even my Siamese cat Zachary turns up his heart-light when I slip him some Tender Vittles to spice up his dry food.

Rewards, sanctions and other influencing factors

A capsule review of behavior mod

Let's go back to a concept we introduced earlier, namely, God as the "contractor." Many believe that God said, "you do this and I'll do that" thereby establishing a contract. It's axiomatic that you motivate and thereby change behavior through rewards and sanctions. Rats run to cheese, pigeons waddle to peanuts, professors publish to get tenure, kids do chores to get the keys to the car and when the judge sentenced Willie Sutton for the third time and asked him, "Willie, why do you keep on robbing banks?" Willie's response was, delivered with a straight face, "because that's where the money is."

There's a flip side to this: flies run from Deet, children from green vegetables, hunters from skunks and the Levin boys from liver. So what were *God's* rewards and sanctions? In Chapter 5, *Why Do People Need God?*, we suggested these rewards could include: protection and safety, a sense of well-being, a refuge from powerlessness, the gift of spirituality and a strong, divine shoulder to lean on. As desirable as these are, for many they are still not first prize for a lifetime of moral behavior.

For many, God's first and highly sought after prize (as Schweitzer remarked) is a ticket to heaven, an "admit one" pass through the pearly gates. And conversely, many have been taught to believe that the flip side of this—for those who take the immoral track—is a one-way ticket to hell. And here's the rub: people all the way from believers to agnostics tell me (hey, they tell interviewers and sometimes, their religious leaders, too, but behind closed doors) that this fear-based bribe is one of the most troublesome issues for them.

I find it both interesting and ironic that more jokes are told about heaven and hell than any other religious topic. They're even in joke books written and published especially for pulpit practitioners. Going further, as we demonstrated in Chapter 6, most people take these two destinations *literally!* From the time they are small children, they visualize a flaming pit for hell with temperatures hot enough to melt your fillings, the devil dressed in red with pitchfork at the ready. The alternative vision has become a permanent wrinkle in our gray matter—that of the pearly gates, St. Peter manning the guardhouse, puffy white clouds and angels strumming harps of gold. Of course, for the radical Islamic bombers, 70 virgins are standing by for each male entrant. One unresolved issue: the imams are not clear about what or who lies in wait for the female bombers. Surely not 70 eunuchs.

Just up the road from Chapel Hill lies Duke University where, in addition to other departments, schools and disciplines, they have a School of Divinity. Thus you might think the last name such a place would choose for their athletic teams would be...*Blue Devils*. It does give one pause for thought. Apparently, "les Diablos Bleus" were a crack team of courageous French soldiers

who fought the Germans in WWI. Units of them even toured the U.S. to raise money for the war effort. Thus, when Duke set about to choose a name for athletic teams, Blue Devils garnered early support but then wiser heads (it was, after all, a Methodist campus) decided it was too controversial. A student vote was taken, but it was inconclusive. In 1922, the editors of the school newspaper, the *Trinity Chronicle,* said..."the hell with it, let's get this show on the road." Surprisingly, the administration, long thought to be stuffy if not pedantic, raised not an eyebrow, and thus, Blue Devils it was and will forever be.

Other believers who do not accept heaven and hell literally may conceive of them as the value of the reputation they leave behind on earth. Their thinking may be that a moral life is rewarded with a warm and kind memory of who you were and how much you did for others: the Golden Rule in action, doctrine transformed into deeds or *orthopraxy*...right living. Hell, on the other hand, would ostensibly be the absence of any good memories about you. The kind of person who is never mentioned at family reunions, and of whom no faded photographs sit on the mantle. But regardless of how you define these two end-states, the very fact that you think about them at all validates their importance as part of the reward-punishment clause in God's contract.

Now, there are a lot of theologians and scholars who believe that a careful exegetical (critical) analysis of the texts in both biblical testaments does not support the popular views of heaven and hell—and certainly not the fundamentalist views on any side of any aisle. Still others, after having sifted through the evidence, cannot bring themselves to accept the pitchforks, 24 hour furnaces or angels-with-harps scenarios. Moreover, many people who do not believe in a spiritual God reject any concept of afterlife as well; accordingly, the traditional concepts of heaven and hell have no relevance for them, though they may very well appreciate the ideas of reputation and memory. And finally, an increasing number of people across the board see heaven and hell simply as metaphors for what happens during your life right here on earth.

Put another way, if you live according to the Golden Rule, your life on earth *should* be "heavenly"—i.e., full of good, true and non-judgmental friends who stand ready to help you in times of need and who offer you respect and love with no strings attached. That is heaven on earth! With regard to hell on earth— there's no need to kill more trees in an attempt to describe it. The words speak for themselves.

Your belief in God:

Continuous, continual or ?

My 10th grade English teacher, Miss Golden, was sorely vexed trying to get me to understand the difference between *continuous* and *continual.* Let me assure you she was not the only teacher who had problems with me.

It was only when she redefined *continual* as *intermittent* that the light finally dawned. Now that we've defined our terms, let me pose the question: does God require you to demonstrate strong belief continuously or will intermittent do? The history of God has a sufficient number of "intermittent believers" who drifted away and then returned.

Which brings us to David. Yes, I know—the popular image is the gentle shepherd, playing the harp, then taking on Goliath with his sling shot—the list goes on. But the darker side cannot be denied: David was a compulsive liar, a conniver, an adulterer, a mercenary fighting against his own people and finally a murderer. He failed in his faith again and again, would repent, then do it all over again. All the while, God never held back his forgiveness and love for David, calling him "a man

after my own heart." And David became the greatest king of Israel.

My reasoning is: if God can forgive a David for all his "backsliding," then surely he would forgive us lesser intermittent believers. But does he? Will he? This is one place where those who believe in a non-spiritual God may have a leg up. At least, they can survey their situation, ask questions, observe the reactions of others and by so doing get some sense of whether they *have* been forgiven. For the rest of us, though, it's a matter of faith.

Now I have a question that plagues me. Is it *normal* to go from strong believer to moderate to nonbeliever, then perhaps back the other way? Mathematicians might call this a sine wave belief. (I suspect any of my former colleagues who see that spelling of sine might smirk and remind me it's also spelled "sin," but in this context, the letter spelling is problematic. So sine it is.) Can't see it? Just think of the edge view of a piece of corrugated tin roof with its curly up and down waves.

In any event, I have met a lot of people whose belief in God looks like a sine wave. One day fervent, one day moderate, the next day distant or worse yet, dysfunctional and so on. I've also met people whose belief in God peaks at the moment they face a life threatening crisis. The traditional movie version of this shows a bigger than life tough guy who never said a prayer in his whole life, falling on his knees in a moment of dire peril, looking up and asking for help. We talked about that in Chapter 5, *Why Do People Need God?"* and called it "being under God's care, protection and safety."

If I had told this story in my classroom, my students would have countered with, "how does it work in the real world, Professor Levin?" In the real world? My guess is that God is an "averager" and takes the longer run view. And I see my God, your God, anyone's God as approaching human behavior in much the same way that a parent evaluates her child's behavior. If the little guy has a bad day, or a bad week (or in more serious cases, a bad year) that doesn't mean that he or she is on the road to a life of evil. It just means that the behavior of kids is often of the sine wave variety, and just as God did with David, we have to take the longer view. But there are exceptions—just as I believe there are exceptions in God's view of human behavior. After all, when he found out what was going on in Sodom and Gomorrah, the biblical God didn't level them right away. He pleaded endlessly, begging the inhabitants to change their ways. But when it was clear after a reasonable length of time that no "behavioral sine wave" was likely to occur, the Old Testament God took the torch to both places. In much the same fashion, I think God averages your long run belief before deciding to take action. Having said that,. I also think that if God gets the impression that your belief surfaces only when you are knee deep in problems of your own making, you are liable to hear from him straightaway and the news may not be good.

God, religion and human behavior

Wrap-up

- God motivates us humans toward normative behavior—a moral pattern that exemplifies the Golden Rule. And if you believe in a spiritual God, he does this by giving humans spirituality that in turn brings out the best in them. If you believe in a secular God, you believe that you and others, acting in community, can help move one another toward the same normative behavior pattern.

- Membership and participation in organized religion has very little to do with moral behavior per se, but *can be a catalyst* if you are ready, willing and able to transform words into action...to walk the walk. People who don't believe in God, but who are moral, are still "good guys." It's all about living the word, rather than just studying or reciting or reading it Over time, religion and morality became separated because of *behavior,* not because of belief.

- Finally, in all likelihood, God is a God of judgment, yes, but then, we all make judgments everyday, about decisions, weighing whether to do this or that, and as we grow in the world, we're being evaluated by our actions. Evaluated by whom? Family, friends, colleagues, neighbors, and that's just for openers. No, God does not sit behind a bench glowering at us over half glasses, like one of those Dickens characters in the Court of Chancery. Nor is he a squinty-eyed, pinched face bookkeeper, hunched over scraps of paper on which meaningless numbers are scrawled in a cramped hand. No...the God who loved and forgave David is not obsessed with the nickels and dimes of our lives. (He might even have had second thoughts about the *Book of Numbers!*)

A closing thought: it has occurred to me that if God had written a business plan for the model known as *Homo sapiens,* I doubt that the core objective would have been the imperative "be successful," or "be famous," or "be powerful or smart." No, I rather think the qualities of being fair, courageous, compassionate, sharing, thoughtful, honest, loving and forgiving would have come at the top of the list. I would also like to think he imprinted these in our DNA—or at the very least intended to. Perhaps the plan was that we would observe those who love and nurture us, and from their words and deeds, we would learn what right living is: *orthopraxy.* Let's be honest—we don't have the franchise on this: After all, wolves and swans mate for life and are faithful, not to mention wonderful parents as well.

Some of the same qualities we were talking about. And they don't even know God. But I think God knows *them.*

My guess is—to use an MBA metaphor—I don't think the day's receipts mean very much to God, nor do the quarterly figures...I believe he is an *averager* who doesn't take snapshots of our moral behavior or what we believe at any one time. I think his real concern is...how does our bottom line add up at life's end?

CHAPTER 9

WHY DO SO MANY PEOPLE USE INTERMEDIARIES TO COMMUNICATE WITH GOD?

R emember the 15 million intermediaries we told you about in Chapter 5? To recap—by intermediary, we're referring to a person who serves as your uplink to God, your primary contact, a facilitator. And after having spoken to a lot of people about this, I can report that surprisingly few people go "direct." In this chapter, then, we'll take a hard look at dealing with God through such an intermediary.

They come in all shapes, sizes and ages, some sporting colorful plumage and others drab—a little like birds. They carry various names and titles, differing levels of authority (and vulnerability) and salary levels ranging from bare subsistence to the obscene. Baptist preachers are *called.* Methodist ministers are *sent.* Rabbis are *hired.* Priests are...well, you get the idea. Whatever the mechanics of getting them there, over the long span of time, there have been millions of intermediaries who have tried to bridge the gap between what are commonly called "lay people" and God. They serve as kind of "go to" persons, if you will. I don't think they function as gatekeepers because I believe God is approachable by all; nonetheless, they are house managers—"God's house." Those in old line declining denominations are sometimes referred to by some scholars as curators of ancient museums. Harsh but fair. However, in addition to their management duties—which in smaller congregations can run the gamut from calling the copier repairman to choosing the right color to paint the bathrooms—they serve as spiritual and personal advisers/counselors and, of course, conduct worship services.

Some faiths grant more authority to the leader than do others. In Catholicism, priests not only function as lay psychologists, in the confessional, but also as God's "interpreter" giving divine forgiveness. Sins are measured by their severity, and the appropriate penance dispensed. They can also grant absolution, sometimes called the remission of sin. By contrast, in Judaism, as a result of the Destruction of the Temple in Jerusalem, sacrifices came to an end, and the need for priests along with it. In rabbinical Judaism, the rabbi's primary role is that of teacher, and he or she is specifically enjoined from functioning as God's intermediary. The rabbi has no power to forgive sins; that is a three-way process among the individual, the party sinned against and God—a dynamic in which God does not forgive you until the "injured" person forgives you. Naturally, the rabbi conducts religious services, but in his absence, any Jewish adult—a person over 13 who is a *Bar or Bat Mitzvah* (Son or Daughter of the Law) can conduct the service.

Islam works a little differently. The imam is a teacher and does individual counseling, too. He leads prayers, but any lay person past puberty can do that also. The imam cannot forgive sin because only God has that power, but the imam can and does teach congregations how to ask for repentance. The imam's sermons are on both secular and religious topics, and in his absence, the person deemed to be the most righteous leads the service. Sounds like a very effective criterion by which to pick leaders of more organizations. In certain other denominations, the leader not only offers spiritual healing but physical as well. After all, the Bible records that Jesus performed many acts of physical healing, as did many earlier and later religious figures. In fact, from the 1960's through the 80's, faith healers came a cropper on television with productions scripted and produced down to the last amen. (We already mentioned the statistical evidence that suggests prayer is correlated with medical healing.) One of these televangelists (don't you love that word) would put his hand up to the camera lens, then ask the viewer to put his or her hand "against his," and the healing power would flow through the picture tube in a mighty cascade of electrons. Though there is no statistical evidence that this worked to generate healing, there is a *lot* of evidence that it generated scads of money.

Still other religions have no formal religious leaders. Urantia, which we introduced in chapter 4, is one of these. This unique interfaith organization is built upon informal discussions and study groups and fills its leadership role on a rotating basis or by its participants collectively. There are no formal services as such and absolutely no clergy or liturgy. Many Urantia participants also belong to more traditional Christian denominations or are Jewish.

In this regard, we would be remiss if we did not mention the Quakers, and their amazing founder, George Fox. In the mid 17th century, Fox took his message to Puritan meetings in England: one should be honest in business and compassionate to the needy. Among his maxims were the ideas that attending a university does not make a minister, and that people, not the steeple, are the true church. His message began to take hold, but as was the case with so many other religious pioneers, there was a price to be paid. He was thrown down

**church steps, beaten with sticks and once even pum-
meled with a brass-bound Bible. Fox was imprisoned,
as were others of his followers, and some of them hanged
in Boston for their commitment to religious liberty.
Originally called the Society of Friends, their bodily display of enthusiasm earned them the nickname, Quakers. In a relatively short period of time, there were
350,000 Quakers worldwide, half of them Africans. Silence was the golden mean in their meetings, and when
the spirit would move someone, that person, man or
woman, could get up to speak. In this manner, thought
Fox, the "inner light" could make itself evident.**

Channeling for God

What draws people to the "slippery slope?"

First of all, let's define our terms. By channeling, I mean
speaking for God instead of speaking *about* God. Very few religious leaders except Catholic priests would ever state openly
that they have the power to speak for God. Reasons for denying
such power might include modesty, prohibitions in the dogma
or lack of total candor. But past and present history suggest they
are presumably channeling for God. Of course, many is the
preacher who has stood in the pulpit and proclaimed with fervor, "God is telling me right now" and then go on to tell you
what God is telling him. Sometimes the message is bland and
other times, it is what is traditionally known as "fire and brimstone."

**A woman came home from church one day and her hus-
band said, "Well, what was his sermon topic today?"
"Grace," she said. "What'd he do with it?" asked her
husband. Her answer came back: "He beat us over the
head with it."**

I'm sure that's the exception, but, "preachin" as it's called down South is heady stuff. I'll set the stage for those of you who may not know: the preacher has the attention of his flock for an hour or so, though the actual sermon time is shorter. But for that period, he is on center stage. He may be wearing a robe and stole, or simply a dark suit, though in the more charismatic non-black churches, the garb may be simply khakis and a sport shirt. In charismatic or Pentecostal black churches, often an organist will punctuate the rhythm and cadence of the sermon with little harmonic figures or riffs. The pace and power of the language will vary widely in churches, from edge-of-the-seat dramatics and spellbinding delivery to a monotone guaranteed to take you to dreamland. But one thing nearly all preachers share in common: they are jealous of their "pulpit time" and guard it, uh, religiously. And it's easy to see why. Like I said, this is heady stuff. Every eye in the place is fixed on you (at least, those that are still open). That's when a preacher can fall into the channeling mode and start speaking "for God."

How does it happen? Well, just imagine yourself in the role of the leader, up there in front of 400 people, mindful of your obligation to help all of them toward application of the Golden Rule. If you are good at what you do, the congregation has come to expect guidance, goal-setting, truth, justification, rewards and motivation all packaged into a 20-30 minute sermon. So with all of this on your plate—on in your goblet—you're very conscious of time; you watch for fidgeting (an early warning signal) as your delivery reaches near escape velocity. And at some point in that process, if you're not careful, the line between speaking for yourself and speaking for God becomes ever finer. Of course, not everyone crosses that line, but lots do. You see, the words carry much greater authority if you say, "I'll tell you what God is saying to me," rather than "here's what I think you *should* do"—and then you go on to tell them. The danger is: once you start speaking *for* God, it's a slippery slope. Does the pressure of time play into this? Is the momentum almost self-generating? Or when people climb into the pulpit, do they seek maximum legitimacy for their message by adopting the role of God's "co-author?" (Obviously, not every religious leader would fit the above scenario, but I think many come close.)

Then there's pastoral counseling. A hurting, confused, needy congregant makes an appointment with you, and once again, from what I've been told, it's easy to slip into the "speaking for God" trap. She says, "Preacher (pastor, imam, rabbi, father) what do you think God is telling me to do?" Oh man, that opens the whole thing up, and before you know it, you're speaking *for* God but using your own thoughts and words. As Joan Rivers used to say, "Can we talk?" We better—because this is where that line we spoke of earlier can become hopelessly blurred.

Thus far, I don't think I've said this is bad, so let me step up to the plate. At a minimum, it's potentially *misleading.* I could also toss in *confusing.* Worse, your preacher could be flat wrong. Worse still, he could be play acting for God, but using human reasoning...a sticky wicket indeed. It does happen. So let's ask the question again—is it bad? You're darn right it is. Maybe dangerous is an even better word because unless that religious leader trying to play armchair Freud has his head on straight, and his theology cleaned up, the parishioners who come into his study confused, doubting and or/searching may well leave worse off than when they walked in. And of course, if he's going to channel for God, what's left for *God* to do? A friend of mine who knows about things like this and who occasionally serves as a pastor's pastor has a technique he uses when he sees someone who, consciously, perhaps unconsciously, is taking his flock down the wrong road by claiming to speak for God, or at the very least, giving them only part of the story. Often, what is left out can be as misleading as what is put in.

Dear Frank (or Dear Joan)

This is just to let you know that I don't need a speech writer. Also, you are not ultimately irrevocably, totally responsible for everything and everyone in the world. That's my job.

Love,
GOD

He tells me that most of the time it works. Now, zoom out to macro and let's picture a televangelist who is on stage in front of 1000 or so people, but whose larger audience may number in the hundreds of thousands. This kind of dynamic can be a powerful aphrodisiac (not in the popular meaning of the word). Then, he gets to the "laying on of hands" and "commands" God to "heal," or its two syllable variant, *HEE-YUL!* delivered with a decibel level that is mind-numbing. (Maybe that's the plan.) You probably know that these "shows" hit major cities in the South and elsewhere. In fact, in one large South Carolina venue, an informed source told me a well known practitioner of the art took in close to $700,000 in three days. Mostly cash, some checks and no credit cards at all. The buses poured in from all directions. Once into the event, the "invitation" was given, and people came up on the stage, some lame, others on oxygen, with walkers or in wheelchairs, with all sort and manner of ailments, many serious, some terminal. The laying on of hands took place, the people fell backwards, were caught, (by yes, assistants trained as "catchers") then returned to their seats. There were *ooh's* and *ahh's* galore. Was anyone healed? That's an open question, and we'll leave it dangling like a participle. Monday morning, the show packed up in the wee hours and was off to the next city before the sun ever cleared the horizon.

Since we mentioned the "laying on of hands," this might be a good place to shed some light on this practice. In Roman society, well before the advent of the Christian

church, the laying on of hands was a time-honored ritual. When a baby was born into a Roman family—whether born to the father or his daughter or even to one of their slaves—the infant was brought to the head of the household, the *paterfamilias,* for his inspection. He looked at the baby and if he liked what he saw, he laid his hands upon the child, in effect saying, I have accepted you into my family. However, if in his judgment, the infant did *not* pass muster, it was immediately removed from the house and disposed of which often meant being tossed upon a garbage heap at the edge of town which was frequently visited by roving packs of wild dogs. (Yes, life was brutal.) This ceremony was eventually adapted to "certify" those applying for acceptance into the church (a larger family). As you might expect, it was the Emperor who laid hands on the first Pope, but within the span of 70 years, it was the Pope who was laying hands on the new emperor.

Making contact with God

Do you need an intermediary?

Assuming you have enough faith, I don't believe you do. But there are lots of people who feel that a stronger connection takes place in a religious service, and preferably, one led by a certified, licensed, ordained, real time (or what) religious leader. Why is this? The answers may include failure to set aside enough private time with God, feeling inadequate, laziness, or just plain habit. Some attend services because they need an authority figure—someone to say when to pray, when to genuflect and when to pass the plate. And then there are those who apparently believe that the very act of their presence at an organized service brings with it public confirmation of their faith or piety and a stamp of authenticity that private conversations with God (that's what prayers really are) cannot achieve. I wonder where ideas like this get started.

In the long history of God, a lot of theologians and major personalities have bemoaned the fact that too many people hold to the attitudes just stated. *If you're not a belonger, then you're not a believer, and God doesn't like that.* Hooey! But then, how did religion become a group activity? We talked about that earlier but a brief recap might be helpful. People do have a need for the kind of guidance that the group dynamic provides, and a shared sense of common purpose and mission strengthens the individual members. That much we know. On the other hand, and interestingly enough, it was Jesus and any number of prophets who would often go into the desert in order to be alone with God.

Of course, collective worship also has social and business values. Oh, yes, folks. It is not uncommon for the long-established religious institutions in a community to be known as the one to join "because you can make some good contacts there." But bottom line—there is no law, no commandment from God that you must be a joiner in order to enjoy him—to have a relationship that nourishes your spiritual self. And you can sit in the back yard under a tree, in the quiet of your study or 8,000 feet up in a plane and think creatively about finding a God that fits you. Take it from an old—but not so bold (anymore) pilot.

On the other hand, we are and always have been social creatures, and it is a fact that people of similar ideas, values and beliefs seem to coalesce naturally into something called community. Come to think of it, one of the most popular Thanksgiving holiday songs is, "We gather together to ask the Lord's blessing."

I'm hardly anti-group or anti-gathering, and for the record, I don't want to see those 15 million religious leaders out pounding the pavement in search of gainful employment. By its very nature, a force that large inveighs against change. Most folks find a measure of comfort in being led and having the worship service laid out for them, so I don't anticipate any earth-shaking rumbles in this area. But let me tell you what I do find interesting, if not puzzling. Information technology, a powerful factor in almost every area of human endeavor, has left organized religion untouched. Are you surprised? I was, too, so let's zoom in.

Our Luddite state

Worship is still done pretty much the way it was even before Cadillacs had tail fins and the Correcting Selectric typewriter had barely reached the drawing board. I'll admit sound systems are better, and the weekly bulletin is smudge-free and the type more legible, but that's still the technology of a previous generation. The fact is: today, just about everything written about religion, God and God surrogates is available on the Internet. (Actually, just about everything written about *everything* is on the Internet. There is a search engine (as amazing to me as Oz was to Dorothy) called "Google" that accesses nearly 3 billion websites of information, each one like a giant bookshelf in a library. When we had a sore throat, Mom used to ask us boys, "did you gargle?" And with today's kids, it's did you

Google? And yes, there are computer programs to help you raise money, keep track of names and addresses and financial contributions as well as programs that provide a treasure trove of filler, anecdotes, heart-tugging stories and biblical commentaries for sermon preparation—even the sermon itself (for a price). If you didn't already know that, then don't embarrass your pastor or rabbi by asking. It's now possible to see and hear a face-to-face sermon in practically any religion even on a palm-held device by any religious figure at any time in any religion's holy scripture.

Using the Internet, you can call up prayers for any occasion instantly. And it's possible for anyone to tailor-make a God concept from among the thousands of God concepts out there simply by adding and/or deleting. Yet—and I am amazed—we continue to use up way too much gasoline to get together for an hour or so each week with others, who may or may not share our religious mind-set, while we listen to one person interpret God for us. We sing songs from numbered references, we read the same standard words together we've always read, we comment on the sermon, observe what some others are wearing, say hello and goodbye to friends and then go home. It's as though this thing called information science had not been invented yet. Are we in this Luddite state because computer strategists don't see God as a growth market, or is everybody just deliriously happy with the way things are—or what? My take on this: there will always be those who prefer a quiet walk in the woods with God, just as there are those who flock to the pews. And just as "distance education" leaves out some important dimensions of the learning process, I fear that "worship-by-wire" may be at best, marginally satisfying.

Should religious intermediaries value-contaminate?

Or should they remain benign or neutral?

Yeah, I know, another word invention of mine. Contaminate is such a loaded word these days, I have to apologize. None-

theless, value-contamination is the act of someone's superim-
posing or interweaving their own personal beliefs onto a given
body of knowledge in order to influence others. Compare it to
using a colored transparency in an overhead projector to under-
lay the data with a tint, a pastel hue. Parents do this all the time:
we call it "teaching our children manners and morality." Psychologists and psychiatrists do it as well, and we pay them handsome fees. Physicians, attorneys and consultants do it also so
why should I single out religious leaders?

Let's look at how it works.

- Parents value-contaminate by passing on their values
  to their children; it's an old accepted tradition and has
  biblical, physiological and psychological credentials.
  You can even find God's blessing for this in scripture.
  (Check out Deut. 6:5)

- Psychologists and psychiatrists value-contaminate but
  only within the bounds of accepted health research and
  practice.

- Physicians value-contaminate patients by adding
  knowledge they have gained from clinical practice to
  their foundation in medical science.

- Lawyers do it by using the phrase, "I would suggest,"
  but they do it in the context of common law and legal
  precedent, and probably a good bit of malpractice insurance too.

- Now when religious leaders do it, they speak for God;
  they overlay their personal values on God's values
  (there's that color transparency I mentioned above);
  they embellish God's words with their own words,
  views and values and therein lies the difference. By
  doing this, they actually alter a sacred value system.
  Ah, but Dick, you say, they are only interpreting what

God said to make it easier for the rest of us to understand it. That's fine with me *as long as it stops right
there!* As we pointed out, however, it's a slippery slope
from interpreting to speaking directly for God, which
is, in fact, changing God's values. And changing them
in a way that may be potentially damaging—even dangerous. Look at what David Koresh did in Waco!

You can readily see why it's a good thing for a physician to
add her own clinical experience to a regimen of treatment she's
prescribing for you. But a religious intermediary is faced with a
different dilemma: it's just not *kosher* to speak for God unless
you *are* God or his chosen spokesperson. Watch out, it gets sticky
here. The difference between an intermediary talking about God
during a sermon and speaking for God (as if he is God) is enormous and the concurrent risk for those of us who are listening
may shove us into the red zone. You see, believers carry a certain concept of God in their minds—a divine composite or alloy—that's been very carefully constructed over the years; and
we've crafted it with care and love and done this on the basis of
what God has believed, said and done throughout his history.
Channeling puts that relationship at great risk by changing its
fundamental contract so that now, what was a two-part relationship between you and God suddenly morphs into a *three-part*
relationship, among you, God and the channeler. Granted, the
changes and alternations might be subtle, but in something this
fragile, one small crack could easily turn into a San Andreas
fault. And you could wind up with a faith-quake.

When a religious leader channels for God and puts his or
her "pulpit spin" on it, a moral code thousands of years old is
being "contaminated" by the individual moral calculus of one
person. Now, the person doing this may be a moral individual—
one would certainly hope so—but that's not the point. Rather
it's that this ancient code, in all its richness and texture and
breathtaking scope will be subject to "tilt"—like the pinball
machines of yesteryear. Having said that, remember that the Earth

is set on its axis to spin at a precise tilt, and should that angle of 66.5 degrees vary even the slightest, the results would be catastrophic. There's plenty of other work that intermediaries are trained and equipped to do so let's take a look.

The mission of the intermediary:

Adding value, not changing God's values

Let's begin by saying that most religious leaders do add value to their congregation through the normal current of the day-to-day activities. What may prove useful for us is to get out of the red brick box on the corner and think innovatively about ways that enhance and strengthen the understanding (and therefore, contributions) of the religious leader without getting him or her into boundary disputes with God. Accordingly, here are a dozen ideas about how best to enhance the real world productivity of religious leaders without stepping on "God's toes."

1. **Outside matters:** The real mission field or parish lies outside the building, beyond the doors. It could be around the world or just around the corner.

2. **The service:** All too often, vibrancy and conviction are conspicuously absent. God should never be dull or repetitive.

3. **Religious counseling:** Only a fraction of those who have questions about their faith ever come forward to seek answers. More need to be encouraged to step out in their search for that God that fits them best.

4. **Young people:** The "graying of the pews" syndrome is hardly any secret. Our hope, and therefore God's hope, lies in helping our youth develop a God concept that can change and strengthen as they grow.

5. **Making religion relevant:** Relating religion to the decisions that people face every day so that it becomes a working tool to help people make better choices.

6. **Tolerance:** We need to learn to accept what others believe or do not believe. God is neither doctrinal nor exclusivist.

7. **Religion and moral behavior:** There is a vast difference between these two, and the relationship is either absent or unclear in too many minds. If you claim to be religious but live immorally, there is definitely a problem.

8. **Finding a God that fits:** In your search for a God that fits, it is not a theological stretch to believe that God is most likely in favor of this search. He may always have been.

9. **Strategy:** Membership, brick and mortar and buildings don't count. What probably excites God's heart more is the individual and collective morality of the congregation.

10. **Flexibility:** Strength of belief is not measured by how many verses you can recite or accept. The true test of faith is how your moral behavior and service to others grow.

11. **Don't be afraid to step on toes:** Making it painless for people to be truly religious doesn't help them in the long run.

12. **Honesty:** Preaching about God with conviction, sincerity and humility wins out over sugar coating or recapping God' s words.

Fifteen million people speaking out about God is a bunch. It's almost twice the population of Los Angeles! Or 1,500 times the population of Jerusalem in biblical times. And now the question: do we *really* need all of these people bumping into each other and coming between us and God? Probably not, but unfortunately, that has been institutionalized almost forever. However, it would seem to make a great deal more sense to reposition more of them *behind* us, pushing us toward God. Sometimes with a shove, other times with a gentle nudge, but always there. However, whether they're in front beckoning, or behind, pushing, remember, as with David, your relationship with God is not a matter of the head, but rather one of your heart.

CHAPTER 10

NINE QUESTIONS TO ASK YOURSELF ABOUT YOUR GOD

My wife, Charlotte, and I love good movies. That's why we can't forget going to see *Armadeus*. And *Places in the Heart* with Sally Ann Field—that was a breakthrough film for John Malkovich as the blind chairmaker. And who can forget Jack Nicholson's unforgettable role in *Terms of Endearment* not to mention Shirley MacLaine. That great scene where they're having lunch and Jack gives her that sly Nicholson stare and says....

Anyway, all that was about twenty years ago. I remember because it was about that time during an examination by my physician and friend, Buddy Harper, that he began asking me this series of questions: Dick, are you thirsty most of the time? Do you urinate too frequently? Is your skin dry and does it become infected easily? And what about shin spots, brown circles about the size of a dime on your legs?)

I answered yes to most of these, having no idea where the conversation was going, until Buddy told me I probably had

Type II diabetes. A few hours later, a blood test confirmed his diagnosis. Fortunately, I have been able to control it with diet, exercise and oral medications, and I don't have shin spots. Now don't panic—I'm not going to recommend that you put down the book and run out to see your physician. The point is: by asking the right questions that in turn led to a blood test, Buddy was able to diagnose the problem, and the result is that today, I am 20 years older and still in good health.

Let's think further on this: what if your relationship with God began to generate "symptoms?" Is there a test you could give yourself? My diabetes test was quick, painless and produced immediate therapeutic benefits. If only the "God relationship diagnosis" were the same, but alas, examining your relationship with God can be long, often painful, involves considerable uncertainty and may not provide any immediate benefits, at least not discernible ones. And even if your diagnosis is successful, changing direction can't be done with oral medication—moreover, there are hurdles to clear and considerations: personal, family, resources, your religious affiliation and more.

Still, there is a self-diagnostic you can run. All relationships give off symptoms as to their health, and marriage counselors among others are adept at quickly recognizing these. The process in the case under discussion will involve determining whether your relationship with God is well defined or just a handful of vague ideas. Accordingly, our questions are aimed to start you thinking about whether you and your God represent a good fit. We've chosen nine, but there are obviously others that could be posed. And this exercise actually has two goals: first, the examination itself and second, to reassure you that self-diagnosis is a good thing to do. Good because it's healthy for your spiritual well-being. Again, God gave us a brain not simply to fill our skull cavity, thus, it's doubtful he would disapprove of what we are doing. Remember those people in the 11th and 12th centuries who thought God couldn't be understood by anyone other than scientists and philosophers. It is precisely that kind of intellectual arrogance that I suspect gives God the human equivalent of a headache. Enough said: let' s begin.

Question 1: How much time do you spend thinking about who or what God is?

We'll approach this from three perspectives. First, if you spend little or no time thinking about who God is, then maybe you've already decided. But step back for a different look: Often we block out difficult or unpopular issues because facing the pain of analysis (or the potential results) is too tough. Silly you say? How many people put off going to the dentist even after the symptoms are plucking your nerve endings like a five-string banjo. It's the same with some people regarding God. Conclusion? If you spend little or no time thinking about God then (1) you may already have an answer, or (2) you may be blocking the process of discovery. You decide.

Alternatively, suppose you are spending too *much* time examining your God concept. Is this even possible? Sure: people often spin their theological wheels and can't get traction. Perhaps your method of analysis is wrong. It occurs to me that to be genuinely effective, an exercise of this sort can't be accomplished in time fragments stolen off the clock. For instance, if your focus on God concept is largely limited to the proscribed one hour a week as part of a formal service, it's unlikely you're serious about God. *Well, Dick, you say, how much time is enough?* The answer can never be quantitative. Remember what God said when asked who he was: "I am what I am." The appropriate corollary here is "you'll know when you know."

Next: should you ask for help in this process? With something this critical, it would be wise to seek input from informed others. It should help you avoid excessive stumbling around in the dark; I say "excessive" because there will be some stumbling no matter how impressed you are with your IQ scores or how much clock time you invest. Thus, outside input is fine, whether individual or group, but in the case of the latter, remember: you are not looking for a God that fits *them,* but one that fits you.

Question 2. Are you able to explain your concept of God to others?

That begs the question: "why should I have to?" Fair enough, but we need to differentiate between "explain" and "justify." A former professor once cautioned me never to try explaining something I didn't already thoroughly understand. If that sounds like just another scholarly aphorism, don't be misled. You'd be surprised to know how much more is said on college campuses than is actually known. Or as Mark Twain said, "It ain't ignorance that hurts but that people know so much that ain't so." Remember, when you start out explaining your God concept to someone, you are not asking that person to believe, but merely to *listen.* And if you find yourself tongue tied in the attempt to explain, then the concept as it resides in your conscious thought may be muddy at its core and at the periphery, drawn with faint, squiggly lines. Put another way, if someone asks you to explain your concept of God, and all you can muster is "God is *something* up there—or (God forbid) the gelatinous word "whatever" escapes your lips—you have your work cut out for you.

Let's take a breather: *if* you know yourself to be a happy, productive person. Someone of strong moral character, who observes the Golden Rule, then you can stop worrying about explaining God to others. It's clear to me that though you may not have a well-developed concept of God, it doesn't affect your behavior adversely. And it probably isn't bothering God either.

Having said that, let me write this large: most of us are *not* operating at our potential and are *not* totally moral; thus, we keep looking to God for guidance and help. And when queried or challenged, it's useful to be able to explain our God in simple and specific terms. In fact, if you think you're clear about who your God is, try writing it down in fifty words or less. If you reach 5 and get stuck, there is some religious or theological house cleaning yet to be done.

Question 3: Are you comfortable with your present concept of God?

Notice I said *comfortable* not *complacent.* Complacent means you've put your brain on hold or into what I call "couch potato" mode. (There are pew potatoes as well.) In either case, real growth has come to a standstill. On the other hand, being comfortable means you've thought about it carefully, deliberately and honestly. Sure, a few questions may remain about doctrine, the liturgy, the openness and responsiveness of God to your prayers, your position regarding various myths and miracles, your feelings about God's revealed behavior and other tones and shadings of your belief system, but essentially, you're comfortable. But then, *how* comfortable? It's like our earlier question, "how much is enough?" It pleases me, though, to see these questions raised because it means people are focused on this issue and they are concerned.

So again, *how* comfortable? Comfortable enough that almost all of your questions have been answered to your satisfaction—but, *uncomfortable* enough to keep working on those remaining that may be causing some mental squirming (that's all right—squirming is good for the soul). Comfortable enough to embrace your God concept with vigor and yes, even passion, but uncomfortable enough so that you'll stay in the study group whose mission it is to explore alternative paths one's journey might take. It's good to be a disciple, but at the same time, make sure your discipleship is open, probing and rigorously self-honest.

Additionally, you need to be comfortable with how your fellow believers view all this and evaluate (dare we say "judge") you for taking this step. We've already mentioned early in our journey together that organized religion has often looked un-kindly at those who question religious dogma. Did I say "un-kindly?" That's being, well...*kind.* In fact, historically, even battles over even conflicts over the very physical presentation of the words (let alone what they mean) or mere ink on paper have often assumed the dimensions of a major battle, and vio-lent persecution became the order of the day.

In the mid 15th century, when Gutenberg began print-ing his first Bible, the Church, having a vested interest in the business of "copying" that was largely done by monks, put out the word that any Bible printed by a machine would be devoid of the spirit of God and must therefore be regarded as the work of the devil. More-over, anyone who read such a book would be damned to hell. Later, in 1525, there was still no printed Bible in English. An Oxford scholar, William Tyndale, to escape the king's and clergy's prohibition, went to Germany to complete his translation of the New Testament. Cop-ies were smuggled into England, and immediately the king and clergy prohibited their use. The church au-thorities bought all they could find and burned them. Undeterred, Tyndale started on the Old Testament and had barely gotten through the Pentateuch when he was betrayed and imprisoned in Belgium. He begged his friends for a warm coat, his Hebrew Bible, a grammar, a dictionary and a candle that he might see to continue with his work. Finally, he was tried as a heretic in 1536, strangled, buried, then dug up and his body burned. He died with the prayer on the lips, "Lord, open the King of England's eyes."

I was at first shocked then saddened to learn of these events, but then, such was the paranoia of the religious authorities. Vari-ants of this kind of behavior have taken place down through the centuries, and even today in some quarters, it's an either-or proposition: either you accept the whole package, doctrine, dogma, rituals and all else, or you don't belong. Quite apart from your private thoughts about God, if any of this kind of judging bothers you, that in itself should be a clue that all of your needs are not being fulfilled.

> **In the year 2000, with the Pope's approval, the Vatican released a document called *Dominus Jesus,* asserting that Christianity is the only true religion and the Roman Catholic Church the only true Church within Christianity. (Does this sound a bit like the Inquisition?)**

Question 4: How well does your God fill your needs?

Abraham Maszlow, the father of modern social psychology, maintained that we have five sets of needs, starting with the most basic, *food and shelter.* Once that has been satisfied, we then aim for *security*—assurances about our future. Then comes the need to be with people, our *affiliative* need. After that, we look to satisfy *our ego need* or accomplishment—and finally when all the other needs have been met, we focus *on self-actualization* (being all that we can).

Although the good professor didn't examine specifically what we need from God or how God could help us fill the five needs, we can do that ourselves. First, if you believe in a spiritual God, it's easy to see the connection between spirituality and self-actualization. Our other needs from God might include being a source of help, strength and support, a sounding board, a confidant, a motivator, a calming influence and a protector.

Using this list and Professor Maszlow's, it should not be difficult to go through a mental check-off and see how well your God is doing filling the needs you've listed. You need to be reasonable, though, and not expect God to be there on a moment's notice waiting to do your bidding. God is not the genie of mythology let loose from a bottle, nor is he Santa Claus. Also, you need to consider that if the only time you really spend with God is that one hour a week, I'd say the linkage between the two of you is tenuous at best. Finally, it's worth remembering that God the contractor said, "If you do this, I will do that." If you're truly living the Golden Rule and carrying your end of the load, and you get no sense that there is any response on God's part, it's probably time to take this up with him. And if that doesn't work, maybe it's time to examine some alternatives.

Question 5: Do the liturgy and ritual you are involved in fit well with who or what your concept of God is?

Put another way, could the God you have in mind have said the words and done the things you are reading? Or for that matter, could the God you have adopted have said *anything?* Does the tone of the language you're reading as you sit there, accurately capture your sense of who or what God is? Is the warmth of the service a good analog of the warmth of the God you are thinking about? Or as we said in Chapter 1, are you day dreaming in parallel during the service about a God who is absent from what is going on in front of you. Granted, these are difficult questions, but necessary for you to ask...and answer if you're serious about finding a God that fits you!

You and I know it's not possible to design liturgy and ritual that would completely satisfy all those billions involved in organized religion. You get a good sense of this if you have lived (or prayed) through a major change in the design, content or thrust of your book of worship. You get an even better sense if you ever served as a member of the group that is doing the modifying. In the first place, the list of people involved in such a venture (usually found near the beginning of the book) is a long one. It involves lay people as well as religious leaders (I would make a joke about the blind leading the blind if I could accurately identify who the blind are). And the list can't leave anyone important out or there will be much wailing and gnashing of teeth.

Chances are this is not the same process God used when he handed down the Ten Commandments to Moses. Coming back to what might be termed religious "trench warfare," to come up with a revised book of prayer, many compromises have to be made, all factions heard and anyone with real power has to be "handled." Consequently, the finished product with accompanying music, ritual, pomp and processionals is a consensus product at best. (I don't know who said it first, but it's a fact that in all the parks of the world, no one has ever seen a statue built in honor of a committee!) At the end of the day, is this process likely to produce something that fits you just right? Hardly. That's one of the flaws of "one size fits all" which seldom if ever seems to work in religious institutions. Of course, minor disagreements are no reason to move on; in fact, I think you need to treat it like a marriage. A good marriage involves a lot of disagreements over everything from is the coffee too strong, you're being too soft (or too hard) on the children and all the way up to which car and which house to buy. But you evaluate a marriage over a long period of time, not day by day. The question is never, "do we quarrel?" or "do we do things that cause each other grief?" Those answers are givens. What really matters is "how has it been for us over 50 years?" If the answer is "perfect" then one or both is playing fast and loose with the truth.

Remember, we suggested that God was an "averager." Marriage evaluations are done in the same way, and this should apply to your finding fault with details of ritual or liturgy. If you get worked up over a word here or a gesture there, that's not being inquisitive—it's being petty. If, however, the entire production leaves you cold, that's a sign you need to think about making a change.

Question 6: Can you handle the myths and miracles that come packaged with your God concept?

Most spiritual God concepts involve myths and miracles. If the God that quickens your heart involves these, can you accept them with naturalness and honesty? Or are myths a speed bump large enough to slow you down every time you think of God? A lot of people feel very close to most of their doctrinal faith except when it comes to myths and miracles. If so, it often helps to see them from another perspective, and if you'll recall, we tried to do that earlier in the book, but a few words about them here might prove helpful.

To begin with, myths and miracles have two historical roots. First, they're part of an expanded adoration of someone. We invent stories about people we love as a sign of respect, and these tend to become embellished as time goes on, enlarged in dimension until these myths and fables have taken on a life of their own. In its own way, it's a wonderfully warm and human way of remembering and celebrating someone's life and accomplishments—and nobody gets hurt. Some biblical scholars believe that a secondary benefit of these was to win followers—build the membership. Sort of a "my miracle can top your miracle" promotion. "Wonder Bread builds stronger bodies 8 ways!" We laugh at that but once upon a time, apparently a lot of mothers believed it, and human psychology seldom changes. To my knowledge, very few faiths insist that you believe literally in every myth and miracle as a condition of accepting God. Being stuck theologically on one or two miracles that have you scratching your head is not reason enough to change your God concept. Come on—you could have won the American League batting title last year with .367. On the other hand, if the dogma, ritual and liturgy seems to be flirting with fantasy, then it's time to do some serious thinking.

Question 7: Do you find yourself disagreeing with God's behavior?

We've covered this earlier and more than once. God has done some questionable things, one could even say "horrific"— or at least, allowed or overlooked them. Blended in with these are his wondrous works as well. I've heard—I have to believe the same would hold true for most of you—hundreds of sermons that rationalize God's behavior when it's immoral, or when it appears to overlook evil. Sermons that make excuses (not apologies) for the inconsistencies in God's behavior, and sermons that twist and pull logic like taffy as they try to explain away why God did this or didn't do that.

Can you accept the Old Testament God's brutality, murderous acts and inconsistency? Or, as the case might be, can you accept the New Testament God standing by as millions are killed in a systematic program of extermination? Does that kind of a God sit well with you? And when religious leaders make excuses from the pulpit for God's sanction of abhorrent (at the least, aberrant) behavior, does it make you distinctly uncomfortable? Would *your* God really behave this way? Are you tired of making excuses to others for this kind of behavior? In fact, what are the limits of behavior you would accept from your God—or is it open season, where anything goes?

Only by asking these questions can you run that self diag-
nostic we spoke of earlier. Remember: you aren't obliged to
accept a God that flies in the face of strongly held beliefs or that
condones behavior you cannot accept, or that makes you uncomfortable. In Chapter 4, we presented a variety of God concepts for people who are searching, and it may be worth while
for you to review these.

Question 8: Does acceptance of your God require you to put your intellect on hold?

Most of the problems—indeed, most of the opportunities—
we face in life yield to our intellectual horsepower. We reduce
threats and we exploit opportunities by applying our brain-power.
If we have to suspend critical thinking to accept God, something is wrong (in fact, a lot may be wrong). God called us to be
faithful and compassionate, but I don't believe he called us to
be stupid or to walk through the valley of the shadow of death
with our brain turned off. Nowhere does it say or even hint that
when you think about God, you should suspend all mental activity. Taking up these questions with God directly is your right.
Your obligation. Thinking about God should never make you
intellectually uncomfortable.

Despite my best intentions, this is starting to sound like a
sermon so let me sum it up simply: if you were in a life-threat-
ening situation, and your brain was sending you survival messages, would you disconnect it and disregard the input? The
answer is obvious. Don't shrink from thinking critically. Don't
cower in fear. Don't cloak yourself in feelings of unworthiness
or low self esteem. Intellect should never conflict with faith. It
should support it. And when it doesn't, you have choices to
make.

Lots of very intelligent people, some with Ph.D.s in everything from astrophysics to zoology, think about their God—
deeply and passionately. And God, who may be the most
important concept in their lives, *needs* to be thought about with

their full intellectual horsepower on line. This holds true regardless of how many degrees you have or whether you ever got out of high school. So go ahead. Give your God a good going over. He can withstand any examination and he can survive any test of logic, but you must be honest and bold. To do less than this is to dishonor God, and I am appalled at the number of people who know better but behave in this fashion whether behind the pulpit or in the pews. Who lets them get away with it? Shame on those of us who do!

But suppose you *do* reject a spiritual concept of God as being antithetical to your science? Fortunately, there are lots of other non-spiritual God concepts you can envision, and you're not alone in this. The difficulties of comprehending a spiritual God weren't discovered last month. We've mentioned those elitists who thought that only a select few could comprehend God. The rest, they said, had to turn off their brains and be buried alive in decaying dogma up to their necks. People like our 16th century Bible translator, William Tyndale resisted, fought back and died to bring truth to light.

> **So for you scientists reading this, you know very well that not everything can be explained by a formula or mathematical function. In statistics, for example, there is an unexplainable variation in regression analysis (try not to wince) designated in formulas by the Greek letter epsilon.**

- Plant pathologists find it difficult to explain the source of the exact placement of ears of corn around the stalk.

- Oncologists cannot explain why some patients with identical tumors live 6 months and others 6 years.

- Yes, and then there were those 56 medical trials in which a statistically significant (translated: it goes beyond "chance") relationship existed between prayer and the medical outcome. The brilliant British physicist, Stephen Hawkings, has proven that the universe is expanding. And if the rate were .00000000001 nanoseconds (I think that's enough zeroes) slower or faster, our solar system would either implode or be blown into smithereens.

If you think science has all the answers to mankind's problems, take a moment to think again (while God has a good laugh). The fact is: in everyone's life, science and spirituality meet up; and at that intersection, you need to pause and take note of your surroundings, check the traffic flow of information and ideas. Who knows what you may see or hear or find? When you get there, if you find your intellect has become hostage to a belief trapped in doctrinal or legalistic gridlock, then set off in a new direction. Remember what Frost told us about those two roads diverging in a yellow wood. Well, there are a lot more than two. God gives us choices. Not to worry. It is the inescapable and irrevocable condition of what it means to be human.

Question 9. How well do you handle change?

Watch your step—this is where the road gets rocky! Changing a God concept is not all that easy. First you have to let go of something before you can grab hold of anything else, and some folks are just not comfortable doing that. Please understand— I'm not talking about a local switch from Baptist to Methodist, walking out one door and in the other. With all due respect to both, the theological difference is about the thickness of a human hair. And I'm not talking about going from imam A to imam B or if preacher A or rabbi B goes to church C or synagogue D, do you follow him or her? If you do, the building may be different along with some new faces, but that's about it. No, the kind of change I'm talking about is much tougher and far more profound: a sea change in the very bedrock of your belief system. Even a move, if you must, away from your God to *no* God. But whatever direction you choose, you'd better be prepared, because you'll have to adjust the controls on your comfort level.

You may love the new setting or...you may find you were better off where you were. Or that neither alternative is the answer.

So why even do this? Well, it's like your annual visit to the optometrist. He puts that device against your face and starts switching lenses. "Is it clearer this way...or that way?" Face it: the reason you are even considering change is that you want to see God more clearly. You want your vision improved. You're tired of "looking through a glass darkly."

Fuzzy and vague outlines and shapes don't cut it for you anymore. For you, nothing less than spiritual 20/20 will do. Good—then go for it!

Change. Some of us thrive on it. Military families that move every two or three years for their 30-year hitch appear to acclimate to it quite well. Their kids blend into new schools; the family finds a house, a supermarket, a place to worship (probably). Others of us cringe at the thought of changing anything: toothpaste, cars, newspapers, the well worn sofa, even our brand of milk or motor oil. Truth to tell, we would do about anything *not* to have to change. Suffice it to say, the challenge of changing a God concept surpasses any of these by an order of magnitude; and the resulting discomfort can last a lot longer than it takes to find the best dry cleaner in a new city. It's a move that should not be taken lightly; it's a move that takes planning and patience, but it's also a move that, if it works, can bring you enormous inner peace, satisfaction and...yes, joy.

- Rule number one, though: before you make the move, be uncompromisingly honest with yourself in sizing up the chances of pulling it off.

- Rule number two: if the risks outweigh your sense of what the benefits might be down the road, skip it.

- Rule number three: consider more than one alternative. Choices allow change and change can lead to personal growth. Remember, it's moral, it's legal, it's honest, it may be healing and best of all, I suspect God will approve.

"the Lord had said to Abram, 'leave your country, your people, and your father's household and go to the land I will show you'...so Abram left..." *(Genesis 12:1 ff)*

CHAPTER 11

DO WE EACH NEED
OUR OWN GOD?

That statistics professor is back again.

In the United States, there are about 190 million people who attend religious services (though their frequency of attendance is in some question). If we leave out combinations of God concepts and non-believers for a moment, but only to make a point, then these are the only four God concept choices available: anthropomorphic God, spiritual God, God surrogates and secular God. Now, suppose the professor asks, "what is the probability that all 190 million people can be satisfied with one of these four unmodified choices?" I must confess, that although I can calculate the probability of drawing the right card to an inside straight in poker, I am completely in the dark about the mathematical answer to my own question here. My intuition, however, tells me that the answer is near zero.

Leaving statistics aside and depending more on our intuitions, let's think about the answer with a series of easy questions. What's the chance that you'd find two out of 190 million people with the same fingerprint? What's the chance that you'd find two women out of 300 attending church services next Sunday wearing the same dress? What's the chance that you'd find two people where you work with the same personality? What's the chance that Americans would be satisfied with only three TV channels? You already see where I am going with this. In each case, the answer is zero or near zero. So ask yourself, why should so many people be pleased by so few choices when it comes to God concepts? The answer is not surprising. They shouldn't. And it turns out, they *aren't* either. Having said that, I'll ask you how many times you'd heard someone of marriageable age say, "I just know there's someone out there who's right for me." Point made. There *is* a God for you!

Let me share a story with you. I'm a fan of *casual empiricism* as a research methodology. It sounds fancy, but it's a cousin to plain old horse sense. It means that you, and maybe a few other folks, decide to look at alternatives carefully, ask some questions, make some tallies, compare your results and come to a conclusion. Not elegant, but quick, and for many purposes, quite effective too. Before radar, U-2 spy planes, AWACS, drones and global positioning satellites, battlefield generals used casual empiricism to estimate enemy strength, although they didn't know it was called that. In the Civil War for example, generals would send out several scouts to see what the other side was up to. When they all returned, they'd compare notes, share impressions and reach a consensus on troop strength. Spy satellites would have yielded a much better answer, but hey, scouts were all they had. Sometimes, an enemy sniper would pick off one of the scouts, and the generals were forced to make their estimate with fewer samples. Today, researchers call that *drawing inferences using small sample statistics.*

Some of my friends and I have been comparing notes lately about how many people affiliated with a religious organization believe in a single, unmodified God concept—you know, one of the four we mentioned above. Our consensus is that 70% of the people believe in one of these concepts. (In this case, all of the scouts got back.) If my arithmetic is correct, that means 30%

of people modify a God concept to fit themselves. Funny thing is, though, if you are sitting in a religious service attended by 500 people, and if you spend the entire time looking around (remember, *casually)* to gauge what God concept people are relating to, you can't pick out the 150 "modifiers." You get no clues whatsoever. Unlike the frown on my face when someone offers me a helping of lima beans, people just don't give off visible signs about their God choice. I'll go you even one better. I'll bet you my last cold beer that if you sit through a dozen religious study group discussions on various topics, the notion of how and why to modify God concepts never comes up.

Why does our multidimensional society discriminate against modifying God concepts?

In the first place, if we're correct in our estimate that 70% of people are satisfied with one of the standard, unmodified God concepts, the majority is clearly in charge, and we are used to that being the case. Then too, consider how we would conduct a religious service if everyone sitting there in the pews had a different idea of how God related to what we were doing. It's sad but true that *standardization* has become a pillar of organized religion, if for no other reason than "crowd control."

But even though standardization is applied to all forms of organized human activity, people still find ways to adjust, modify, add to, take off, re-do and tailor-make their lives so that their highly individualistic tastes can be satisfied. The designer clothing business is huge. Most people alter standard house plans to suit their individual needs. Cars can be ordered in a bewildering array of colors, engines and accessories. College students can choose from hundreds of courses, and you can purchase men's shoes up to size 24 EEEEE. (I also find it mysterious how so many dishes in a Chinese restaurant can come from so few pots. That's something I've never figured out.) And custom-designed furniture has found a big market in spite of its very high cost. Conclusion: we go to great pains—not to mention, expense—to tailor-make portions of our life experience. Sometimes we do it for physical fit, sometimes for aesthetics, sometimes to feed our egos, and sometimes just to make us look different. But when it comes to God, most of us—more than 2 out of 3—revert to "one size (four in this instance) fits all" Strange!

The challenge of designing your own God

Some constraints that make it difficult

As we've alluded to, organized religion has not exactly encouraged experimentation with God concepts. Sure, there have been those individuals who have gone against the grain in terms of liturgy, doctrine, sacraments and the like. In an earlier chapter, we chronicled the fight that Luther waged against the Catholic church some 500 years ago. But in the history of organized religion, reformers and revivalists have been the exception and not the rule. Innovation and God modification are rare members of the species that in its most entrenched form could be called *ecciesiasticus calcificatus.* (Don't bother looking that up.) The fact is, for the most part, no matter how many claims it lays to recognizing and championing individuality, organized religion is a *group* activity. Indeed, if furtherance of individuality were a primary goal, there would be far less pressure (and there is pressure) to attend organized services and far more focus on individual seeking and communicating with God. If they were truly focused on individuality, religious institutions would acknowledge and, one would hope, honor the special needs of the 30%; and there would be formal education in evaluating and selecting God concepts. In their defense, some do squeeze in time for silent prayer in the service, but the message still comes over loud and clear: do it our way. Perhaps that's the price of admission that a society of order freaks has imposed on our inherent need to seek God.

It's an oft-repeated cliché—a repugnant, misogynistic southern aphorism on how to handle a difficult wife—"keep her pregnant in the summer and barefoot in the winter." Can it be that organized religions (and individual faiths, denominations and variations within those religions) sometimes try to keep us in the same state as our poor southern spouse of legend (read that, submissive, accepting, not experimenting, not questioning)? If so, then why? Could it possibly have something to do with market share? Is it the risk that intelligent people who question their current God concept might sail right off the edge of the spiritual earth—like the "experts" once warned Columbus? Throughout the history of God, new religious groups have always been formed out of older ones and faster today than ever. The impetus to leave and strike out on their own has always been dissatisfaction, never satisfaction. People never left because they were pleased but because they *didn't* agree with what was going on. (I must be honest here with history—as I am writing these words, it occurs to me that I am describing exactly what happened with Jesus and the temple, and then later on, between Paul and the synagogues.) Does discouraging consideration of alternative God concepts really protect market share or put it at risk? Should a religious group pay any attention to the 30% and if so, how much? Or is it all just about *control?*

If 30% of their congregations are vetting other God concepts, why don't we see a more positive reaction from God's intermediaries? Would it be unreasonable for more of them to offer the 30% some small measure of recognition? A modicum of understanding and support? Or would that offend and maybe confuse the 70%? I find it curious that even though most seminary curricula contain courses on the history of God (reference our Chapters 2 and 3) post graduate study generally focuses on accepting and promoting only one God concept. I don't think that's a planned tactic—I think it's plain old work avoidance. In the first place, and as we said before, it would be difficult to identify who the 30% are, and they would be a pain in the gluteus for professors since the "outsiders" tend to be more vocal. Who knows? In a congregational setting, if they *were* recognized—better word, accredited—as a significant minority, they might start asking for special services, liturgy and other perks. All of this is starting to sound like extra work and more angst to me. And angst—either for our intermediaries or the congregation—does not make for happy pew sitters or the person in the pulpit, no matter the denomination or faith. Look at what has already happened with gay ordination and same sex marriages.

Speaking of angst, any congregant who even glances sideways at a different God concept can create plenty of angst for himself. First of all, in addition to being flat out uncomfortable with the form and content of the service, our "rebel with a cause" has to strike out on his or her own in order to "discover" others who might share the discontent. You can't really advertise in the temple bulletin. *Wanted: God seekers who are malcontent. No experience necessary.* Sure, to that brave individual, her actions may seem perfectly logical, but the word heretic could be bandied about.

I must tell you this, though it is painful for me as a former teacher and scholar merely to relate it. Several years ago, the president of a well known and highly respected private southern college wrote a brilliant, probing book about how to be open and honest when talking about God. The thoughts put forward were ones in an earlier time that Jesus himself might have put forth; and the tone of the book was respectful, scholarly and highly spiritual in nature. The state organization that "ruled" over that denomination—and this was their very word—called him a "heretic" and threatened to (their word again) *excommunicate* him. If that sounds like a modern day version of the Inquisition...well, we'll let it go at that. The book is *When We Talk About God, Let's Be Honest!*

Examining God concepts to find a better "weave of understanding" should be a normal process. It shouldn't involve any embarrassment or exclusion and should be acceptable to others just as it's acceptable to God. It's not that one is trying to worship or serve another God, but merely finding a different lens through which to conceptualize God. Indeed, as long as a congregation remains in touch and in tune with its members, "brand switching" will probably *add* as many members as it might take away; and I can't think of any reason why it has to be carried on under cover, other than it must be perceived as a threat to the status quo. Pursuant to that, here's a bit of church history you may find interesting.

> **WHEREAS, we, his Majesty's Justices of the Peace in the county of Stafford, have received information that several disorderly persons—among them, one John Wesley—calling themselves Methodist preachers, go about raising routs and riots, to the great damage of the people and against the peace of our Sovereign Lord, the King:**
>
> **THEREFORE, you are commanded to make diligent search after the aforesaid Methodist preachers, and to bring him or them before his Majesty's Justices of the Peace, to be examined concerning their unlawful doings.**
>
> **Given under my hand and seal, this 12th day of October, 1743.**
>
> *W. Persehouse, The King's Magistrate*

This warrant was issued and it is a miracle it was never served, but not because the officials didn't try. And all because John Wesley wanted to offer a different take on worship, a different way of celebrating God, a kinder and more humane way of treating the downtrodden—a segment of the populace all but ignored by the Church of England—while still remaining a vibrant, authentic, deeply spiritual believer. Now you see what I'm talking about.

Ultimately, you must be comfortable with your God concept

If not you, then who else?

If that sounds like a dictum (or what the Vatican used to call a *bull),* then let me explain where I'm coming from. In Chapter 8, *God, Religion and Human Behavior,* we hypothesized that the purpose of God (any God) was to help individuals achieve their full moral potential. Doesn't it follow logically then that if you believe in a God, being *comfortable* with that God is a prerequisite for moving up to the top of the moral scale? Conversely, if you are estranged from your God, motivation is not likely to take place; if you're drifting from one God to another, it's not likely to happen either. And if you believe in God but don't feel that you have God's full support and backing, it's going to be very difficult for you to self-actualize (thank you Professor Mazlow) and behave more morally.

There's another way to come at this. Being comfortable with your God obviates all of the time and energy you'd otherwise spend searching. But be aware: peace and serenity with your God has never meant that it will be easier for you from now on, or that you'll have less to do. It only means that all of your energies can be focused on the goal (moral behavior) instead of on the search.

Put another way, *doing* replaces *searching* and *trust* replaces *timidity.* Be aware, though, of your new commitment, as Paul, the ex-tentmaker puts it, "faith without works is dead." By the way, that phrase, *be aware,* has a special meaning to pilots. When the air traffic controller radios, "8213 Yankee, be aware—" you know that bad news is coming, all the way from "you are flying into a thunderstorm," to "you can't land here today." Being comfortable with your God reminds me of being comfortable with the airplane you are flying. (And I can tell you, I may have thought I knew my Piper Twin Comanche before flying it around the world, but afterwards...well, it was a whole new relationship between man and plane.) What I am saying is that when you learn how and why your plane behaves in a certain manner, you learn to trust it, and when you learn to trust it, that's when you really start to enjoy flying. If we build that bond of trust with God, then the relationship will flourish.

Who's behind you on the sidewalk?

A brief treatise on the nature of risk and trust

True moral behavior always involves risk-taking decisions. Often you have to stick your neck out and do something that makes you really stretch. However, it's known that people will willingly take risks if they have faith in the outcome. I used to do a little experiment with my MBA students. We'd go outside the classroom on the sidewalk and I'd ask for a volunteer. Then we'd tie her hands together (in front of her) and her ankles, station three or four large guys behind her and ask her to fall backwards into their waiting arms. You'd be surprised at the number of those who refused to participate. And these were classmates who knew each other well, who studied together and depended on each other for help. Why am I telling you this? Because if you say you believe in God, but don't trust him to "be behind you on the sidewalk" ready to catch you, it's not likely you'll ever reach your full spiritual and moral potential.

How do atheists and agnostics find trust and faith?

Who's behind them on the sidewalk?

First of all, there's no shortage of trust or faith in their lives. It's all a matter of defining your terms and the source. Sure, they made a choice, and some tell me that periodically they re-evaluate that choice—which was to reject all God concepts. And making the right choice is as vital to them as it is to anyone else. Returning to the question, "who's behind them on the sidewalk?"—they rely on themselves for wisdom, judgment and courage when risk rears its head. Their life experiences have inculcated in them good moral standards. And they also rely on their support group of family, friends and colleagues. I find no evidence that as a group they are less willing to take risks. I touched upon the subject of atheism earlier in the book using a friend as an example, and I'll stick with what I said then. It isn't that my atheist friend on page 161 is not a believer; she *is,* and a strong one. It's just that her belief system is grounded in moral bedrock and simple kindness, not a deity or a being or a set of formal religious doctrines. And like those coal miners Woody Guthrie sang about, "she will not be moved."

This chapter is examining whether each of us needs our own God grounded in a concept with which we are comfortable; and from that perspective we ought to reinforce something you probably already know, or strongly suspect. Atheists and agnostics are not more alike than are people who believe in God. In fact, their beliefs vary widely. Some of them accept biblical personalities for their contributions as teachers and leaders; other reject anything having to do with biblical history. Some of them adhere to very strict moral codes; some do not. Some people become non-believers after being put off by early religious training; others left organized religion after years of comparing actual human behavior and the human condition with God's promises. Some can't even tell you why they left. Do they each need their own view too? Of course they do, and fortunately, America is a society where they can express it openly. (Someone please assure me that it still is.)

Is need for God related to your age?

Isn't everything else?

It would seem so—everything from sex to medicine to cruise ship vacations to easy-open bottles of painkillers and adjustable beds, and of course, healthcare. I once attended a medical conference at which the speaker reported that, on average, 30% of your entire life medical care expenditures came in the last three years of life. On a far more blissful note, I recently read that some people enjoy sex in their 90's. Somewhere between those two extremes, there is probably a happy life for all of us. However, contemplating people's need for God based on their age is more difficult than for sex or medicine.

If we go back to our childhood, for most of us the earliest recollection of God occurred at the age of three, and by that time, the idea of God has been firmly implanted in our minds if at all. If you're at all familiar with human cognition, you know that three-year-olds can't handle a concept as complex as God. Therefore, it's no surprise that most of them are introduced to an easy-to-relate-to anthropomorphic God. Consideration of a spiritual God begins somewhere between five and nine, depending on individual mental maturity.

Then we get to the teen years. Some wag once remarked that as a parent, by the time he and his wife got to the point where they could put up with their son, the son couldn't put up with them. Rejection is the order of the day about the time the glands kick in, and God gets included in the mix. Teen age rejection of God usually peaks at college age, although most often, college students reject frequent attendance at religious services more than they do God per se. Who knows—that may simply be payback for never having been allowed to sleep late on Sundays. The earliest outright rejection of God turns out to be correlated with taking advanced undergraduate courses in philosophy and the like. Now if that sounds like "Levin slams colleges as atheistic," forget it. This is simply a time in the mental and social development of young people when they see themselves as mature enough—though maybe not wise enough—to put a lot of their beliefs under a microscope, God being one of them.

How about from 25 to 50? Credible numbers here are hard to find, but we do know that identification with a God and worship attendance generally strengthen again right after marriage. This could be an expression of support for your spouse, a consensus decision or a search for counseling. Later, when children appear, there's a definite spike. That has its impetus in youth rituals—baptism, Bat Mitzvah and Bar Mitzvah, confirmation and the like. Also, there's the decision to "give the kids something to at least get them started; then they can make up their own minds later." That spike declines slowly until kids leave the home when it falls off more sharply. It's not until the middle years that membership and participation in organized religion takes on a more social dimension and then begins to climb again in the 60s. Researchers attribute some of that to concern over the vagaries of aging and end of life.

These data are averages and as such can mislead you. My favorite "average" story concerns an Air Force recruiter responsible for finding pilot trainees who average six feet tall. He shows up with two candidates, one four feet in height, the other eight feet. The orderly progression of data are also jilted by special events in people's lives which rekindle or fan the fire of belief in God, regardless of their age. For example, it's common to encounter people who find God (or Jesus or any God surrogate for that matter) and this can happen at different ages. What we can say without reservation is (1) that, in general, belief in God *is* related to age and (2) that there are several distinct ages— or lifetime events like college and marriage—at which point belief either rises sharply or falls. (Take another look at Chapter 6 for more detailed data.)

So much for the numbers.

Now what are they telling us?

Or as my engineering professor used to say, "what are the normative implications of what you have found?" What does it mean to know that people change their mind about God as they age? Just this. If individuals, parents, professors, religious leaders and whoever know that belief is cyclical and age-dependent, they ought to be able to respond better and in a more timely fashion. When I was a young parent, I reacted strongly to my kids' use of certain "four letter" words. A psychologist friend of mine told me one day that it was perfectly normal, age-appropriate behavior for kids to use those words, and after that, I loosened up considerably. He was right, too. I have watched each of my three kids in turn as they react to similar behavior in their progeny. Apparently, kids still use the same four-letter words, my grandchildren being no exception.

Conclusion about God and age: if you are willing to do the work required and suffer some of the vicissitudes of the search, there is no single age where finding a God that fits you is best done. There *are,* however, times in your life when the process can suffer from lack of attention, preparation, knowledge and commitment. And remember, if you are really at odds with your God, consider giving him a second chance. After all, he's probably been doing that with most of us from time to time.

The title of this chapter is "Do we each need our own God?" and I hope we've answered that. But to press the issue, how is that need best met and actualized? In what form might we best experience that? Is there a one best way? Herein follows Dick Levin's formula for the ideal religious experience:

I envision this consisting of the ecstatic, unrestrained joy of the *Chasidim,* selected guidelines from Torah law that make such good common sense; the beauty and awe-inspiring wonder of an Episcopal Evensong, the honest and open dialogue of a *Urantia Book* study group, the quiet soul-searching of the Quakers and finally, the pulsing "swing and sway, sing and pray" experience of African-American worship. Right, Dick. That's easy enough to put together. See, that's exactly the problem. There *is* no one best way—there are just lots of *good ways* to honor and celebrate and be faithful and loyal to your God concept—and comfortable...no matter your age, education, bank account, golf score or anything else. Remember, it's because of independent thinking men and women down through the ages that we are offered these choices—to put a number on it, there are over 10,000 religions in the world which tells us that the folks at Baskin Robbins still have a way to go.

Can you find an appropriate God by yourself?

I knew you were going to ask me that.

And I'll just bet you a lot of people asked Mulla Sadra the same question. This cleric/theologian lived in 15th century Persia (its name didn't become Iran until 1935). Sadra was working out his theology about the time our friend Gutenberg was putting the pages of the first printed Bible to bed. And those who came to him for enlightenment and guidance, left with these words echoing in their head:

There is an individual God for each person found in that person's imagination.

For Sadra (and for Miamonides three centuries earlier), imagination as a source of God made sense. In fact, if more people would embrace an axiom like this, fewer of them would have a doctrinal axe to grind. Now, back to my original question: yes, you can find an appropriate God by yourself...but it's not easy. To do it effectively, there is a lot of preparatory work that has to be done: reading, discussion, research, contemplation, casting out, bringing in, and yes, prayer. My experience has been that these kinds of processes work better if you have someone or a small group to work with. Understand, however, this choice of a God that fits you is a very personal decision, and the final choice must *always* be yours. But it sure does help to bounce ideas off other people who may be making the same journey. This way, you avoid blind alleys, especially those the other group members have already encountered. You also avoid being limited by what you alone know, and that's a lesson often ignored by too many people. Better still, a group is able to expand the number of options to be considered.

For these and other reasons, if you can try, find a few others who are seeking—not yet satisfied—who can help you. Look for intelligence, for patience, for reasoning ability, and most important, look for people who are non-judgmental. And equally important, look for people who are passionate about what they believe—whatever it is and who behave morally. If you can't find people like this, you can still reach a successful outcome. Obviously, I don't know how your mind works, but you may need to be more analytical, more organized and thorough and maybe even more disciplined so as not to overlook opportunities or settle for the wrong conclusions. Some meditation doesn't hurt either.

Preview of coming attractions

You are about to turn the page and segue into our closing pages. In Chapter 12, I'll lay out a process that may prove helpful in your search. I'll present eight examples of God concepts designed by people to fit their individual needs. That's only eight out of what can reasonably be a thousand times that many, but it's designed to get you pointed in a useful direction—and remember, I'm big on saving trees. So if you're ready, go ahead and turn the page.

CHAPTER 12

FINDING A GOD THAT FITS YOU

We've been leading up to this point for eleven chapters and now we're here. It's time to put it all into practice, time to look at the different God concepts, consider the pros and cons of each of them and make a choice (or "design" your own). Time to let go a little, view the landscape of ideas and emotions and see if you can find something that excites you...something new that strikes your fancy. Time to take what you've got, add to it, whittle on it, sand down the rough edges and make it fit you. Time to fish or cut bait. Time to stop talking about it and do it.

Again, what are the real alternatives?

So many choices, with time the unknown

Actually, there are only six basic choices, but that's a bit misleading. In fact, the number of combinations and variations is infinite, and that's what makes a choice of God concept difficult on the one hand, but fascinating, beautiful and creative on the other. A story about difficult choices...when I was a little kid, my Uncle Lou had a Frankfort Unity store in Philadelphia, one of those small neighborhood grocery stores where the family lived on the second floor. When we kids visited uncle Lou, he would take us down into the store and to the candy counter, telling us we could each have all the candy we could carry in one hand. Talking about a child's heaven! But the exercise was not as easy as it seemed: there were considerations of type, mass, volume, weight, breakability, ease of holding onto and other factors, including whether uncle Lou was looking or if Mom would make us "put some away for later" when we went back upstairs. So, in case you're a little rusty on God concepts, here are the six basic choices for you to review.

1. **Anthropomorphic God:** a God that takes a human form in the mind of the believer.

2. **Spiritual God:** a non-human form that can't really be seen but which can be experienced. The God of the Old and the New Testament would be one of these. (Sometimes referred to as a *theistic* God or *the God of scripture).*

3. **God surrogates:** A few extremely influential historical figures who are worshipped by large numbers of people: Buddha, Jesus and Mohammed would fall into this classification.

4. **A secular God:** a God that is neither anthropomorphic nor spiritual, but one who dwells in humans and manifests itself by the collective moral behavior of society.

5. **Variations and combinations of all of the above:** God concepts which result from acceptance, rejection, modification and combination of 1, 2, 3 and 4 above.

6. **The absence of God:** Rejection of any and all God concepts.

Variations and combinations

You may be wondering, just how does this work?

For starters, let's take a look at the Druze, a desert sect founded in the 11th century. In later times, the Druze lived about a hundred miles northeast of Jerusalem and fought the ruling Ottoman Turks for a couple of centuries. They are still a tribal and cultural entity in the Middle East today. The Druze combined the teachings of Buddhism, Christianity, Islam and Judaism with the tenets of the Greek philosophers to wind up with what is among the most interesting God concepts in history. Their creed today is basically Muslim. Druze had the training of Roman warriors and the culture of desert-hardy nomads. Though they weren't the first people to evolve a religious amalgam of God beliefs, theirs was surely the most eclectic of the early combinations. Very little was left out!

On the other hand, some people believe in a spiritual God that is totally exempt from biblical origin or biblical history and totally divorced from Buddha, Jesus or Mohammed. In their minds, this God is a contemporary spiritual force they believe can affect human life, a force they believe hears and responds to prayer, and a force they think has a significant impact on earth. This God is an interesting variation of the God of biblical history you and I know about. But who *created* this concept of God, divorced from the more well known God concept? Good question! *The people who believe in it did.* Who creates any of the almost infinite number of possible God concepts? Aren't they in fact all created in the minds of people who then develop or almost "grow" a belief in this seed they have planted?

Isn't that exactly how every God all the way from the very beginning came into people's lives? But does this God hear people praying? The ones who are doing the praying certainly think so. How, then, does this God stack up against the more well known or "traditional" God most people pray to? If you ask people who believe in this "modified" spiritual God, they think he's the most powerful of all. And in the "God business," that's all that matters, isn't it?

Let's try another variation, this time a modification of our old friend, "anthro God." It shouldn't surprise you that some people believe in a *black* anthro God. No old white man with a long beard, blue eyes and rosy cheeks, puffed out as he blows his breath and makes waves, literally. No, this one is a rotund, cheerful, affectionate black man. So what's the big deal? All that has been changed is color, weight and personality. Nothing else from the traditional image is different, and all the biblical imagery is intact. There is no doubt that to black folks, this image of God "fits them." (Let's face it: why would they want an "old white man?") Why the modification? C'mon, that's a no brainer. It makes for a better fit. But does God have to fit to be useful and effective? Hint: the title of the book gives you a big clue. And I suppose that to continue with this new "family" composite, Jesus would have to be black too, but since he was already a Semite with a dark complexion, it wouldn't be much of a stretch.

Now, consider: where did this black anthropomorphic God come from? *Out of someone's imagination, of course!* And why? Because the old white man with the long beard didn't fit. Get it? *Didn't fit!* Well, then, does this concept of God really work for people? Ask a congregant, not me. Then there are people who believe in a very specific segment of society (or of let's say, St. Louis); they pray to a secular God who is the collective conscience of their family (generally, though not always, defined as *extended* family). Imagine God being thought of as being the morality of your family. Hold onto this image—can this God hear prayer? We agreed (I guess we did) in Chapter 4 that a secular God could. Could this God act if it wants to? Indeed; haven't you ever been saved by the actions of your family? Not to mention sanctioned as well? Can this God observe and react? Any extended family can do that. Does this God satisfy followers? I'm not sure I'm the right one to ask, but why not track down someone who believes in a secular God and ask her. (And take notes.)

People who believe in God make adjustments to these surrogates too. It shouldn't surprise you that lots of people believe in Jesus as a God surrogate, but in a Jesus absent of much of the theological baggage normally associated with him. That leaves Jesus as having been just another human being with two anthropomorphic parents. These people pray to Jesus the teacher, the rabbi, the faith healer, the agitator, the provider, the moral standard and the exemplar. (That's a fairly impressive list wouldn't you say?) What about God, then? For some, in this God concept, God may take a metaphorical back seat to Jesus. We talked about that a bit in Chapter 4 if you feel like browsing. But why would someone want to pray to a modified—and much more human—Jesus instead of God? That's easy: they feel closer to Jesus—more comfortable. The word I'm really after is *intimacy.*

President Thomas Jefferson altered the bible to fit his own concept of religion and God. He railed against Jesus' followers whom he felt had corrupted and obscured what Jesus had said. He included in these "corruptions" the virgin birth, original sin, the atonement, predestination, salvation, bodily resurrection and the Trinity. Jefferson said that miracles were an affront to reason and the laws of nature, and consequently that the New Testament was also corrupt. He ordered two copies of The King James version and, using his razor, proceeded to winnow out what he called "the corruption of Paul and his successors."

The President called his new version *The Philosophy of Jesus* of Nazareth. It was about 46 pages long and two columns wide and came to be known as the Jefferson Bible. Since his death, Mr. Jefferson has been variously described as "an atheist, an infidel, a theist, a Deist, a Unitarian, an Anglican, and a secular humanist." To say the least, Mr. Jefferson was not a traditional Christian, but Sadra and Miamonides would have understood.

The verse, "taste and see that the Lord is good" occurs in both Psalm 34 and again, only slightly varied, in 1 Peter 2:3. This I believe lends credence to our thesis: the importance of finding a God that *fits* and is to your taste.

The point is: people see God as alive and as an active person. They feel he hears them and responds. Probably most important, it's a better fit with who they are and who they want to become—*finding a God that fits you.* Should we call this modification anthropomorphic? It doesn't matter what you *call* it—only what it does for your morality, i.e, the way you treat others.

There are quite a few Mystic Christians in the world. And there are numerous variations of belief among this group. Each of these represents yet another modification or combination of the six basic God concepts. All Mystic Christians accept and pray to a spiritual God. And all of them recognize and accept Jesus, too. So far, they sound like mainstream Christians—but wait. Some Mystic Christians reject the virgin birth, the divinity of Jesus, the resurrection and the trinity. Other Mystic Christians accept subsets of these four. They see all this as beautiful myth which helps weave the fabric of belief, but they don't accept it literally. Well, what would you call these people? If they behave morally, I'd call them good religious folk.

Another example of the kind of God concept you can design if you use your imagination and intelligence involves a Jewish friend who believes in a secular not a spiritual God. He does however enjoy Jewish worship services. It provides him a place and an opportunity to meditate. Participation in the service brings him comfort. The songs he sings and the prayers he chants are from his childhood. The sermons tend to be on current issues and are informative and relevant for anyone. When the liturgy references God, he can pray to his secular God without embarrassment. My friend tells me he finds this combination satisfying, and I believe him. The God he has chosen is clearly a secular God, but what I find interesting is that he has put this God into a traditional Jewish religious service. Would God approve? My feeling is that this depends on how my friend behaves during the 166 hours a week he's *not* in the synagogue.

One final example of an individually tailored God involves a middle-age Catholic couple I know. Neither one goes to confession, and they practice birth control. And they both disregarded the meat prohibition back when "good Catholics" didn't do that. They give generously to their church but neither believes in a literal heaven or hell. The God they worship now (a modified spiritual God) has evolved into its present form over a dozen years.

Question: are they good Catholics? Answer: it depends on whom you ask. Ask *them* and you get a very positive answer. Ask their priest and you get a different response. Calibrate their behavior with church dogma and you get still a third view. Why then do they go to the Catholic church? They say they enjoy and benefit from being there. Does God approve? You must have memorized the answer by now: it all depends on how they behave, and from where I sit, they stack up really well on that criterion.

Finding a God that fits

Are there enough choices for me?

The short answer is "yes." The number of choices goes on and on and on. Intelligent people have always created and modified God concepts and it will continue forever. Let's step aside for a minute and conduct a little mathematical exercise. (You didn't really think you were going to get by without this, did you?) In any event, in the mathematics of permutations and combinations (liberal arts majors take a deep breath), you can calculate the number of ways a group of things can be formed into modified groups. Now, I just got through giving you eight different examples of how the basic six God concepts have been modified. If you've had a burning desire for most of your adult life to figure out how many different combinations of 1, 2, 3, 4,

5 or 6 of the basic six God concepts can be formed, voila, here's how to do it.

$$\text{Answer} = 2 \text{ (to the 6th power)} - (6 + 1)$$
$$= 64\text{-}7$$
$$= 57$$

Is this magic? Hardly, but it does tell us that if we take the 6 basic God concepts in their pure form and combine them into groups of 1, 2, 3, 4, 5, or 6, we can get 57 different combinations (Heinz, eat your heart out). But what if we changed each basic group just a bit and then started to put them together in groups of 1, 2, 3, 4, 5 or 6. How many choices would we have now? There are two appropriate answers here: first answer 4,096. Second answer: this is the end of the arithmetic lesson. Point to remember: if you are an intelligent person and have an active imagination, Miamonides and Mulla Sadra were right —there is no real limit to the number of God concepts you can envision. And what *that* means is, if your current God concept doesn't fit who you are (or who you want to be) there are more choices than you can shake a staff at. The only requirements for success here are reasonable intelligence, enough honesty to evaluate your situation objectively, the imagination necessary to conceive of God concepts that might fit you (don't worry about the math) and...oh, we almost forgot—the courage to loosen up on your grip, look around and perhaps make a move.

Are all of these possible choices acceptable to God?

Meaning yours, mine, Aunt Becky's, cousin Joe's....

You already know that I believe God approves of any behavior that makes you a better person and the world a better place. In Chapter 8, *God, religion and human behavior,* we wondered whether God was a behaviorist and whether his methodology was behavior modification to help you become a more moral person. It makes sense, then, that anything that moves you along toward that goal should be acceptable to God. If you examine biblical history carefully, God doesn't appear to be an ideologue when it comes to particular practices or nuances of religion. Quite the contrary, he seems to focus more on what people *do* instead of how or where or how long or loudly they pray, a normative model for all of us, I might add (and sadly). Yes, I believe you can safely conclude that God will approve of any choice you make, conditional upon its enhancing your morality. I even believe God is willing to give you a little time to see if it is working. With all due respect for your concern about God's approval of your choice, I believe your first concern should be making a choice that's good for *you.* It stands to reason—and remember: God loves for us to use the gift of our minds—if you make the right choice, the long run outcome should be pleasing to God.

Will any of these choices offend anyone?

You have to be kidding.

The simple fact that you are even *thinking* about changing God concepts will likely send some people into orbit if the news gets out. As we've touched upon, the process of evaluating God concepts is rarely talked about in organized religion. It surely is not part of any Sunday school lesson, nor is it taught in most adult education classes and it is certainly never heard in a sermon. The God part apparently is a given—something that's fixed, immutable, everlasting and not open for discussion. It's O.K. to change denominations, but change Gods...? Like I said, you gotta be...

This is a journey that takes a lot of faith in yourself, your friends and in your God. It also helps to have a thick skin, a strong sense of direction and plenty of patience. Changing Gods is right up there next to slipping out the back door with the Torah under your coat or having an affair with the priest. I can hear it now: *you're changing Gods? Are you sick or what? Why, you're going straight to*...hello! Is anybody listening to what I am really saying? And remember—thus far, all you've said is that you're merely *thinking* about changing your concept of who or what God is. Now let's consider the biggest bang of all. Suppose it got out that you were thinking of giving up God for...well, for *nothing*. Batten down the hatches and Katy bar the door!

Change is difficult for individuals but it's always more difficult for organizations. When a lot of people get together and arrange things in a particular way that pleases them, they have a problem with people who want to change things around. My friend tells me that in a certain parsonage in Georgia, there is a plaque on the wall that reads, "Do not move any piece of furniture in this parsonage." He did move an ancient, all but worthless chair in the sanctuary, and you would have thought he had challenged the Almighty to a debate. See what I mean? There's even a standing joke among religious groups: how many (fill in the name of the denomination) does it take to change a light bulb? The answer is 9. One to change the bulb and 8 to stand around and moan about how much they're going to miss that old, burnt out bulb).

But don't despair. Lots of things are on your side. First, the fact that you are looking for another God need not be announced in front of the congregation. Your search can be carried on extramurally. Of course, if you're having trouble with that notion, ask your God if it's O.K. to talk with some of his compatriots to see what he (or she) says. Sharing your problems and your journey with your family makes great sense and no one need be the wiser. Getting help from people outside your congregation can work too. Taking your religious leader into your confidence is another thing. Some of them might react positively, others would not. Before you make a move here, you should evaluate this on an individual basis. I may have created a false impression that this process is like picking a movie to see. That's clearly not the case It's a personal and sometimes painful process. It has been for me!

Some people spend years contemplating, reflecting, considering, evaluating and suffering too, often in silence, thus magnifying their pain. Thus whatever strategy you adopt for sharing (or concealing) must stand the test of time. My personal sense is, that doing this all by yourself is probably not the best strategy.

What if my choice rejects all concepts of God?

That's a definite possibility.

If you've been honest with yourself, if you've examined the God candidates objectively, if you've put your imagination and intelligence to work conceiving of modifications and combinations, and you come up empty, so be it! Lots of folks spend years looking for a spouse only to decide that being single is the better alternative. When you reject all concepts of God (anthropomorphic, spiritual, secular, God surrogates and combinations) you have joined the null set as we defined it earlier. When you do this, what or whom do you lean on? Not to worry. About 5% of adults in the U.S. say they are non-believers, and the evidence suggests they would be hard to pick out of a crowd. They don't have horns (like Michelangelo gave Moses), they wear appropriate clothing, they don't necessarily beat their children and they give to charities too. Five percent of U.S. adults is a little over 3 million people, so you should have lots of opportunities to find them, enjoy their company and learn from each other. And whatever you do, don't get paranoid. Remember, the ancient Jews were called atheists for refusing to acknowledge the gods of the Greeks. Finally, no God concept choice is forever; if you want to change, you change. No forms to fill out, no entrance fee, no exam.

Is one process for making a choice better than another?

This is a two part answer.

One: if it turns out you make the right choice, no one cares what process you used. Two: if you make the wrong choice, you can't justify it by saying you used the right process. This seems to suggest that process is unimportant, but that's not the right inference to draw. Process is important; you just can't use it an excuse if you are wrong. So unless you are good at picking the optimum answer from among 4,096 possible God concepts (and remember—that's a low number) the odds are that you should use an organized process for choosing. If your process is flawed, the outcome will probably not be what you need, and there isn't much likelihood of behavioral change. Ergo, there's not much that will happen that's likely to please God or you.

Sometimes it's risky to show smart people how to make complex decisions. I often think of some of my ex MBAs on Wall Street who used complex decision models (including a few I taught them) to pick technology stocks a few years ago. I'm sure they meant well, but nevertheless they lost several zillion dollars for their clients. I wouldn't want the same fate for you.

So, I'm going to make a few simple suggestions on how you might go about selecting (or designing) your choice of a God concept from among the many possibilities available. Nothing magic like how to pick stocks—just a little common sense.

Using a little common sense to make a choice

If you don't start with this, the road gets muddy.

The first step is to make a candid assessment of the time, effort and commitment you are putting into establishing a relationship with your current God. If this comes up short, don't waste your time switching God concepts before you address your lack of commitment. Although it's true that lack of satisfaction *will* reduce commitment, let's agree to get past the chicken-and-egg routine and consider that switching Gods from a basis of weak commitment is not a smart move.

The next step is to define what you believe in now...what or who is the God you pray to, the God you lean on for support? Try describing that God in fifty words, to improve your own focus. Next, I'd suggest you gauge the strength of your belief, say on a scale from 1 to 10, ten being the highest. Are you a consistent believer, a believer who hedges and holds back, a fervent believer, a mildly interested believer or actually more of an *observer* than a believer. Now make a list of the characteristics of your God that attract you, that please you and that satisfy your needs for a God. What are your God's best features?

Now, turn the page over and look at the other side. Which characteristics of your God turn you off. Which characteristics do you find it hard to accept. Which characteristics need some tweaking for you to feel good about them. Which characteristics do you completely reject. Assuming that your commitment is high, one extreme example would be when your belief is at least a 9, when your list of positive attributes is extensive and when your list of negative (or modifiable) attributes is very small. If that's who you are, you're probably among the top 10% of all the people who believe in God, and you're probably a contented person. Assuming your commitment is still high, the other extreme would be when the strength of your belief is under 6, when you have a long list of complaints (unmet needs) about your God and very little to say positively. If this is an accurate description, it's just not working for you and you're a strong candidate for a change.

Is it time for an exchange or a modification?

Defining extremes (as we did in the two examples just above) is easy to do. But most of us don't operate at the extremes—we're mired somewhere in between. And most important decisions aren't found at the ends of a continuum either; they involve trade-offs galore. In this instance, God seekers are faced with these five fundamental choices; retention as is, retention with modifications, replacement without modifications, replacement with modifications and rejection without replacement. (If this sounds a bit like changing spouses, I assure you it's unintentional.)

Retention as is: You give your current God concept a very careful vetting, you examine other God concepts, you ask yourself the right questions, you make comparisons and you conclude that the fit between you and this God is good, it's functional, and it does what you need. So for now, you don't change.

Retention with modifications: After a lot of thought, self-examination and imagination, you come to the conclusion that modifying your God concept can produce one that fits you much better. Accordingly, you modify some of the characteristics, underlying beliefs, myths, miracles and anything else you find unsatisfying or offensive about your current God concept and accept it in its changed form (no rules here, no tests).

Replacement without modifications: Without having to make any modifications to it, one of the alternative

God concepts appeals to you strongly. You examine it very carefully, and it represents a solid match with who you are, what you need, how you think and what you want to become. So you adopt it.

Replacement with modifications: One of the alternative God concepts appeals to you. It's *near* who you are as a person, you believe it could significantly affect your potential, and you believe it could become a very exciting part of your life. But it has a few characteristics that keep it from being a tight fit. You modify these characteristics, whatever they are, and you accept your new God.

Rejection without replacement: The entire set of alternatives is systematically examined. You consider a wide variety of possible modified God concepts, but none of them appeals to you. You reflect carefully on what it would mean to you to reject all of the God concepts and live without God. It makes perfect sense to you and you are excited about the choice, so you do it (no letters, no flags, just happiness).

Useful thoughts to keep in mind in your search

It's short of the list of 613 mitzvot, but then, who's counting?

1. You are not the first one or the only one in this situation. Millions of people reflect on their God and whether that God fits who they are and who they want to be.

2. Thinking about changing a concept of God did not start last week. In our condensed history of God in chapters 2 and 3, we saw that this has been going on from the very beginning.

3. Going through this process is not immoral, it is not blasphemous, it is not wrong, and it is not an offense against God. Seeing you unhappy was never part of God's plan.

4. God will love you just as much when you finish the process as he did when you began, but you may love *yourself* more.

5. Searching for a God that fits you may confuse some people; it may anger others, and it may disappoint family and friends. But you may wind up a better, and more contented, person.

6. Going through this process will not make you a moral person. The best you can hope for, if you're successful, is that it may unlock more of the moral potential within you.

7. Not all religious leaders will understand why you are doing this, and some will try hard to dissuade you. No one ever said, however, that to please God you had to please his intermediaries first. This is between you and your God.

8. You may go through the entire search and still come out unsatisfied. Many people search for God their whole lives and never feel they have found the right one.

9. Using your imagination in this search is critical. Philosophers like Miamonides and Sadra said it centuries ago, and it's still true today: the choice of Gods is almost infinite. The odds are that you can find one that fits you well if you can conceive of who or what it needs to be.

10. The process will fail unless you are perfectly honest with yourself about who you are, what kind of a person you want to be, what pleases you about your God, what antagonizes you and whether you have the drive, stamina and patience to undertake this search.

11. If you do find a God that fits you—as you are now or the person you want to become—the search is not over. You still have to learn to live with that God, to be perfectly honest with him and to trust him.

12. This is not necessarily a choice for a lifetime. Neither should it be a "choice of the month." Even couples in love have a 50% divorce rate. Changing your mind about God is a very human act. Changing it every year is a big mistake.

13. You can lead a very moral life without God. No one has established that you must be spiritual to be moral. There are multiple ways to learn morality, only one of which is a relationship with God.

14. Don't depend on help from your religious leader. Ask for it if you think it's prudent, but don't be put-off if it doesn't come. Seminary training does not generally include courses in this subject.

15. Participating in the normal activities associated with belonging to a congregation may not be the best way to evaluate your relationship with God and to make choices (something about missing the forest for the trees).

16. Don't concern yourself about whether the God you believe in is shared (or even understood) by the person sitting beside you during services. Your bond with that person is not whether you believe in the same God but whether both of you are moving up the moral scale.

17. In the final analysis, you are the only person who must be pleased with your choice of a God. God has already proven he can live with whatever choice you make *as long as your behavior is moral.*

End of the road...for me.

Let me state the obvious: I am not a theologian nor do I have any credentials in that arena. I haven't taken a single seminary course nor do I subscribe to learned journals in theology. But when reduced to its essence, theology is best defined as the study or contemplation or examination of God. And that is the journey I signed on for as your guide. Along the way, I felt rather like Lewis and Clark when they set out on their expedition to find a land route to the Pacific. Accurate maps were nonexistent—little more than guesswork. Or John Wesley Powell, who after having lost an arm at the Battle of Shiloh, decided to map the wild Colorado River as it wound through the Grand Canyon turning from placid pools into a raging torrent.

At times in putting together this narrative, I think I know how Powell may have felt. While navigating the current of my narrative, I encountered rocks and rapids, twists and turns, whirlpools and at times, I was forced to stop and "patch my raft."

I admire your courage in having signed on for the journey and your patience for staying with me. In the process, I've shared with you everything I know (or at least, think I know) that might help you find a God that fits you. It's not a guarantee, you know—not a done deal. It never is. As Yogi Berra, another theologian in the rough, once remarked, "the game ain't over till it's over." Thus, your relationship with God must ultimately be more organic than it is organized. Which is another way of saying, it is in a constant state of growth. It keeps on emerging...evolving into new forms. Alfred North Whitehead, the brilliant English philosopher, said that the reality of autumn was not the colors of the leaves themselves but the process—the fact that each year the colors *would* undergo that transformation. That was something we could count on with complete assurance. In much the same manner, we know we can count on God. Over the ages, as humankind has altered, adapted, polished and ground the lenses through which it sees God, the reality of God is constant. It is always there...like the seasons.

History is filled with the stories of people who have reached their full moral potential with God's help, and others who behaved morally without it. It can work either way. Clearly, it takes great courage to loosen your grip on what may have become routine and comfortable for you in your practice of worship and pursuit of God. This much I do know—life is not a dress rehearsal. So if you hear the distant sound of rushing water, follow it to where it touches the shore...then like John Wesley Powell, launch your raft into the river and embark on what may well be the most exciting journey of your life.

Go ahead and do it...I think God would approve!